The Black Archive #7

THE MIND ROBBER

By Andrew Hickey

Published September 2016 by Obverse Books

Cover Design © Cody Schell

Text © Andrew Hickey, 2016

Range Editor: Philip Purser-Hallard

Andrew would like to thank:

Philip Purser-Hallard, Jennie Rigg, James Brough, Emily Wright, Richard Flowers, Alex Wilcock, Laura Sneddon, Jac Rayner, Andrew Rilstone, Holly Matthies, Bill Ritchie, Richard Jones, the Midnight Folk, and the Mindless Ones for discussions which sparked things in this book, often indirectly.

Also available

The Black Archive #1: Rose by Jon Arnold

The Black Archive #2: The Massacre by James Cooray Smith

The Black Archive #3: The Ambassadors of Death by LM Myles

The Black Archive #4: Dark Water / Death in Heaven by Philip Purser-Hallard

The Black Archive #5: Image of the Fendahl by Simon Bucher-Jones

The Black Archive #6: Ghost Light by Jonathan Dennis

Coming soon

The Black Archive #8: Black Orchid by Ian Millsted

The Black Archive #9: The God Complex by Paul Driscoll

For Holly.

CONTENTS

OVERVIEW

Serial Title: *The Mind Robber*

Writer: Peter Ling (episodes 2-5), Derrick Sherwin (episode 1, uncredited)

Director: David Maloney

Original UK Transmission Dates: 14 September 1968 – 12 October 1968

Running Time: Episode 1: 21m 27s

Episode 2: 21m 39s

Episode 3: 19m 29s

Episode 4: 19m 14s

Episode 5: 18m 0s

UK Viewing Figures: Episode 1: 6.6 million

Episode 2: 6.5 million

Episode 3: 7.2 million

Episode 4: 7.3 million

Episode 5: 6.7 million

Regular cast: Patrick Troughton (Dr Who), Frazer Hines (Jamie), Wendy Padbury (Zoe)

Guest Cast: Emrys Jones (The Master), John Atterbury, Ralph Carrigan, Bill Wiesener, Terry Wright (Robots), Hamish Wilson (Jamie[1]), Bernard Horsfall (Gulliver), Barbara Loft, Sylvestra Le Tozel, Timothy Horton, Christopher Reynalds, David Reynalds, Martin Langley (Children), Paul Alexander, Ian Hines, Richard Ireson

---

[1] Specifically the face-swapped Jamie in episodes 2 and 3.

(Soldiers), Philip Ryan (Redcoat), Christine Pirie (Princess Rapunzel), Sue Pulford (The Medusa), Christopher Robbie (Karkus), John Greenwood (D'Artagnan / Sir Lancelot), David Cannon (Cyrano), Gerry Wain (Blackbeard).

Antagonists: White Robots, Toy Soldiers, The Master [of the Land of Fiction], the Master Brain

Novelisation: *Doctor Who: The Mind Robber* by Peter Ling. **The Target Doctor Who Library** #115.

Sequels and Prequels: 'Future Imperfect' (short story, 2001), *Conundrum* (book, 1994), *Head Games* (book, 1995), 'Character Assassin' (comic strip, 2001), *City of Spires* (audio, 2010), *Night's Black Agents* (audio, 2010), *The Wreck of the Titan* (audio, 2010), *Legend of the Cybermen* (audio, 2010), *The Crooked Man* (audio, 2014).

Responses:

'...conceptually, if not actually, the first post-*Sgt Pepper* **Doctor Who** story...'

[Mark Clapham, Eddie Robson and Jim Smith, *Who's Next: An Unofficial and Unauthorised Guide to Doctor Who*, p114]

'...a nice change after so many bases under siege but ... still a little ropey in places'

[Ray Dexter, *Doctor Who Episode By Episode Volume 2: Patrick Troughton*]

SYNOPSIS

Episode 1

The TARDIS's dematerialisation fails during a volcanic eruption, and **the Doctor** is forced to move the ship 'out of reality' and into 'nowhere'. While he repairs the engines, **Jamie** and **Zoe** see images on the scanner of their respective homes. Zoe runs outside and Jamie follows, but they find themselves in a disorienting white space where unspeaking **white robots** show them sinister, smiling, white-clothed versions of themselves.

Meanwhile, the Doctor is fighting off a telepathic attack from an unseen antagonist, **the Master**[2], who wants him to leave the TARDIS too. Eventually he does, but is able to rescue Jamie and Zoe from the robots and usher them back aboard. They take off, but the Master renews his assault, now affecting all three of them. The TARDIS explodes in flight, ejecting them all into space.

Episode 2

The trio wake separately in a landscape resembling a forest, observed on screens by the Master. Jamie and Zoe are quickly incapacitated – Jamie shot by an English **redcoat**, which turns him into a cardboard cutout, and Zoe trapped in a stone dungeon. The Doctor meets a friendly traveller with an archaic turn of speech, who drops hints about the Master of this kingdom, and six Edwardian **children** who assail him with riddles. He decodes another riddle which has the effect of restoring Jamie, but only after the Doctor has assembled the wrong face for him from a

---

[2] NB Not the Time Lord of that name – see footnote 16.

collection of jigsaw-puzzle features. Otherwise his usual self, Jamie recalls the TARDIS exploding – much to the Doctor's alarm – and also a dream about a unicorn attacking him.

Another riddle turns the door of Zoe's dungeon into 'a jar', from which they rescue her. Climbing a tree, Jamie discovers that the 'forest' is made up of giant letters spelling out proverbs. The trio are arrested by full-sized **clockwork soldiers** in the service of the Master, who take them to a dark space where they face the hostile unicorn from Jamie's dream.

Episode 3

By vigorously asserting the nonexistence of unicorns, the Doctor, Jamie and Zoe turn the beast into another cardboard cutout. Another meeting with the violent redcoat gives them the opportunity to reassemble Jamie's face correctly before entering a labyrinth. The Doctor and Zoe meet **the Minotaur**, who they are also able to eliminate by disbelieving in him, and the Doctor's traveller friend from the forest, who he now realises is **Lemuel Gulliver**, the hero and narrator of *Gulliver's Travels*. The Doctor speculates that they have 'tumbled into a world of fiction'.

Left on guard outside the Minotaur's chamber, Jamie is chased by a toy soldier. He ascends a cliff to escape, and climbs a rope which proves to be the hair of **Princess Rapunzel**. Rapunzel's chamber is in the Master's citadel, where Jamie finds databanks of stories from human history. A ticker-tape machine is outputting an account of the Doctor and Zoe's current encounter with another mythical enemy, **the Medusa**, whose gaze can turn them to stone.

Episode 4

Zoe's disbelief in the Medusa is not strong enough to dissipate her. The ticker-tape narrative provides the Doctor with a sword, but he rejects this solution to their predicament as it involves accepting the Medusa's reality. Instead he shows Zoe the creature's reflection in a mirror, which restores the Medusa to her previous state as a statue. The ticker-tape reports that the Doctor has failed a test.

The Doctor and Zoe are attacked by a superhero, **the Karkus**, who Zoe knows from 21st-century comic strips but who is unfamiliar to the Doctor. Zoe is able to wrestle him into submission, and he agrees to take them to the citadel. There the pair find Jamie, who shows them the ticker-tape machine. The Doctor realises that the failed 'test' was an attempt to turn him into a fictional character by persuading him to obey the narrative. Zoe triggers an alarm, and the white robots take them to meet the Master.

The Master is a hack writer who was kidnapped from Earth in 1926 and harnessed to the mechanical **Master Brain** that runs this realm, his creativity serving its superior, though unimaginative, intelligence. Now elderly, he hopes to recruit the Doctor to replace him. Jamie and Zoe escape through a library, but as the Master's narrative dictates they are caught by the white robots and pressed between the pages of a book.

Episode 5

The Doctor's friends are now fictional characters, and his only hope of restoring their personhood is to join with the Master Brain. He refuse and flees. Rapunzel and the Karkus help him gain access through a skylight to a typewriter which seems to be the source of the ticker-tape narrative. He tries to direct the course of events from there, but realises in time that this is another attempt to fool him into fictionalising himself.

Seeing the Doctor as a villain, the fictional Jamie and Zoe lure him with the help of Gulliver and the children into a fake TARDIS which links him to the Master Brain. The Master reveals the ultimate plan of those he serves: to fictionalise the whole of humanity and thus depopulate the Earth ready for occupation.

However, the Doctor begins to assert control over the realm, freeing Jamie and Zoe from their literary trap and using the Karkus to destroy the toy soldiers the Master sends after them. The Master fights back, and a battle of fictional heroes ensues, with **Cyrano de Bergerac** duelling **D'Artagnan**, and **Blackbeard** fighting **Sir Lancelot**. Zoe and Jamie take advantage of the distraction to overload the Master Brain's systems, and the Master collapses, having ordered the white robots to 'Destroy!'

The robots set about destroying everything in their path, although the Doctor reassures Zoe that their friends will be safe, as fictional characters cannot be destroyed. He speculates nervously that he, Jamie and Zoe – and the Master, now free of control – will be returned to where they belong. They fade away, and the TARDIS is seen reassembling itself.

INTRODUCTION

The Mind Robber (1968) is almost unique in televised **Doctor Who**. The show's original conception had been to have three types of trip through space and time – forward, to worlds of the future for science-fictional excitement; backward, for historical stories which would at least theoretically educate the show's child viewers about the past; and 'sideways'[3]. The 'sideways' stories were not, as that term would now suggest, stories about parallel universes (and in fact it took **Doctor Who** a surprisingly long time to do such a story, despite it now seeming an obvious option for any science fiction series – it wasn't until *Inferno* (1970), broadcast nearly seven years after the show started, that the Doctor first travelled to such a universe). Rather they were stories that involved other states of being, whether miniaturised (as in *Planet of Giants* (1964)) or outside of time and under the TARDIS' mental influence (as in *The Edge of Destruction* (1964)).

Only two of these sideways stories were made before the idea was abandoned, although two more stories featuring William Hartnell's Doctor could possibly be considered also to be sideways stories (*The Space Museum* (1965), largely for its first part, and *The*

---

[3] The original conception for these 'sideways' stories, as outlined in a production memo was that they would be journeys 'into all kinds of matter (e.g. a drop of oil, a molecule, under the ocean, etc.)' (quoted in Howe, David, Mark Stammers and Stephen James Walker, *The Handbook: The Unofficial and Unauthorised Guide to the Production of Doctor Who* (2005), p53), but by the series' third story, *The Edge of Destruction*, they had become more generally journeys into other states of existence.

Celestial Toymaker (1966)). *The Mind Robber* was the first – and only – return to the idea with Patrick Troughton as Doctor, and it went further in this direction than any other televised **Doctor Who** story, playing with narrative and metafictional ideas in a way that was unlike anything the series did before or since.

Seen out of context, in 2016, *The Mind Robber* seems like a bizarrely experimental piece of television for what is, at base, a children's fantasy series. In context, in 1968, as the second story of season six, it was if anything even more bizarre. By this point in the series' history, it had become defined by a simple formula, later given the label 'base under siege' by fans. *The Mind Robber* was Patrick Troughton's 16th story as the Doctor, and 10 of his previous stories (including seven of the eight stories in the previous season) had what amounted to the same plot.

In all of these stories the Doctor and his companions would land in some sort of isolated place which had a large central area consisting of an impressive-looking set (a moon base, a space station, a monastery). Some alien monsters would be attempting to break into the base, and the Doctor and his friends would fall under suspicion of being collaborators. It would turn out that someone already in the base was a collaborator, but was probably being mind-controlled by the monsters. The Doctor would defeat the monsters, using some schoolboy chemistry or just sheer pluck and cleverness, and then he and his companions would leave.

That formula had become what **Doctor Who was**, in the eyes of the viewing public, and while *The Dominators* (1968), the previous story in season six, hadn't followed the formula exactly (for once there was no base), it was close enough to it that it was still comfortably familiar, at least to those viewers who weren't put off by the story's general crassness.

So when episode 1 of *The Mind Robber* was first broadcast, it must have seemed truly shocking to viewers. Rather than a safe landing in a research facility that was being besieged by killer robots, the TARDIS materialised in... nowhere. Blank emptiness, with no other people anywhere.

That blank emptiness, it turns out, was more to do with the show's budget than with a desire to change from the formula. *The Dominators* had been cut from the originally-planned six episodes down to five, due to a dispute between the series' production team and the writers, and so *The Mind Robber* had to be extended by an episode. And this, more than anything else, was what made *The Mind Robber* the unique story it is.

The new episode, you see, had to have practically no cost. There was no budget for actors with speaking roles for an extra episode, the sets hadn't yet been built, there was no money for any new costumes, and so other than the core cast (Patrick Troughton as the Doctor, Frazer Hines as Jamie, and Wendy Padbury as Zoe) the show had to be made using only the pre-existing TARDIS sets, four robot costumes made for another programme and operated by non-speaking actors, and a completely blank set.

The resulting episode, written by the show's script editor Derrick Sherwin rather than Peter Ling, the author of the rest of the serial, gave the story some much-needed menace and suspense. Over the coming chapters we shall see how creative responses to production problems such as this came to define the story, and turn it from something that could have been a mere retread of *The Celestial*

Toymaker into a story that almost uniquely from Troughton's era stands up today as a piece of inventive, groundbreaking television.

Many of those creative responses were the work of a new director. David Maloney, who had worked on the series before as a production assistant, was just starting in his directing career, but as we'll see throughout this book, he brought to the role a visual imagination that was far beyond the run-of-the-mill direction with which the show was usually encumbered.

Over the course of this book, we will examine the extent to which each of these creative minds – Sherwin, Ling, Maloney, and the cast, along with producer Peter Bryant – contributed to what may, 48 years later, still be the single most experimental **Doctor Who** story ever broadcast on TV.

The Mind Robber is a story about authorship, about the border between fantasy and reality, about the imagination, and about the way characters can seem to take on a life of their own. It's a story written by someone who never wrote another **Doctor Who** story, and it's utterly unlike anything done in the series before or since, yet it is one of the stories that is most admired by fans, and seen as an example of what **Doctor Who** is capable of at its best.

In this book we will look at this unique example of 1960s **Doctor Who** and the circumstances of its making; at the surprisingly deep questions of authorship it asks, and at how those questions of authorship can themselves be asked about *The Mind Robber*, and to a lesser extent about other **Doctor Who** stories. Is *The Mind Robber* a bizarre exception, or is it the furthest extreme of a continuum, with more in common with the stories around it than first impressions would suggest?

15

THE PRODUCTION

The Mind Robber was the last story to be made in the production block of 46 episodes which had started in season five with *The Abominable Snowmen* (1967), nearly a year earlier. During that time, the show had had two producers (Peter Bryant and Innes Lloyd), two script editors (Bryant and Derrick Sherwin), and a change of cast, with Deborah Watling departing 30 episodes into the block and being replaced by Wendy Padbury as space teenager Zoe Herriot from the story *The Wheel in Space* (1968) onwards. Despite these changes, the production block had been remarkably consistent in style. Almost every story was some variant of what has become known as the 'base under siege' formula – a formula that had been developed by Gerry Davis and Innes Lloyd during the previous year, and which would be used off and on for much of the series up until the present day, although as of yet never to the same extent as during season five.

But the formula was wearing thin, and so as the block drew to a close, the current production team of Peter Bryant and Derrick Sherwin, along with Sherwin's assistant Terrance Dicks, were looking for a way to vary it.

So when Sherwin and Dicks found themselves discussing **Doctor Who** with fellow writer Peter Ling, as they travelled between London and Birmingham for meetings about **Crossroads** (1964-88), a soap opera on which all three were working, Ling's lack of experience with science fiction didn't matter:

> 'During that time, when we were all commuting to Birmingham, I got to know them and they suggested I write a **Doctor Who** story. My first reaction was "Oh no, I couldn't

possibly do that, it's not my cup of tea, and I don't know anything about science fiction." In the end, I did what must have been one of the least science fiction orientated stories they made.'

Ling was initially asked to come up with ideas for a six-part story, but his idea, for 'the vague notion of a planet inhabited by fictional characters, on the supposition that everything has an existence of its own and must go on living somewhere, in some direction of time, space, or thought' was initially commissioned as a four-part story under the title 'Manpower'[4]. Bryant and Sherwin were enthusiastic about the idea, and Sherwin made a few suggestions for how the story could be improved, notably suggesting that Lemuel Gulliver only speak in lines written by Jonathan Swift in *Gulliver's Travels*, rather than in normal dialogue, and replacing the 'brain creatures', the rather unimaginative token monsters Ling included in his original breakdown[5].

However, after Ling delivered the four-part story, the production ran into a problem – *The Dominators,* the season opener, was being cut from six episodes down to five, and so *The Mind Robber* needed to expand by a similar amount, without any additional budget for sets, costumes, or speaking cast.

Sherwin quickly wrote a new opening episode, tying in to the volcanic eruption at the end of the previous story, in which the

---

[4] Howe, Stammers and Walker, *The Handbook*, p261.
[5] Howe, Stammers and Walker, *The Handbook*, p262.

TARDIS crew find themselves in a featureless white void[6], populated only by unspeaking robots[7], and Jamie and Zoe are shown visions of their homes, and see visions of themselves, in a trance and dressed differently, before the TARDIS itself breaks up and they find themselves clinging to the console, which is spinning silently through black, empty, space.

A mere description, in text, can't really convey the unnerving effect of this episode, which has to rest entirely on the acting ability of the principal cast members, all of whom carry it off wonderfully.

But what's interesting to note is how many **narrative** purposes the new episode manages to serve. As well as providing a bridge between the 'real' and fictional worlds, it also manages to suggest the possibility that all that follows is taking place in the characters' minds, rather than in a physical location. Ling's original idea had been to have the story set on 'a **planet** inhabited by fictional characters' (emphasis mine), which may have seemed slightly twee and unbelievable. Adding in this hallucinatory opening chapter

---

[6] In one of the few disadvantages of being able to see the story in DVD quality, with a clearer picture than it would have had on transmission, the featureless void appears, on the DVD release, to have rather obvious joins between the wall and the floor. These are unlikely to have been visible to viewers on broadcast.

[7] The robot costumes already existed, having been created for an episode of **Out of the Unknown** (1965-71), a science fiction anthology series. They were merely repainted for their **Doctor Who** appearance, and thus required no significant additional budget.

moves the action to something closer to the Platonic realm of Forms, outside normal space and time[8].

This allows those of us who are comfortable with such stories to take the action of the story as 'really happening', while also providing the possibility of an 'and it was all a dream' reading for those who are wedded to a purely materialistic, rationalistic, view of what **Doctor Who** is meant to do.

At the same time, it provides a link back to an older tradition of British children's literature. *Alice's Adventures in Wonderland* (1865) has a similar dream logic, explicitly explained at the end of the book as being the protagonist dreaming, and Jonathan Miller's then-recent (1966) TV adaptation of the book shares a hallucinatory quality with *The Mind Robber*, and especially with its first episode. But *Alice* is merely the most prominent example of a whole strand of fantastic children's literature which includes the work of CS Lewis, E Nesbit, and many others, several of whom have been cited as influences either on this story or on **Doctor Who** as a whole. Tat Wood and Lawrence Miles say in **About Time**:

> 'More than any story before or since, *The Mind Robber* has the sense of **Doctor Who** repaying a huge debt. There is [...]

---

[8] Though never named in the story itself, this realm has become widely known among **Doctor Who** fandom and in tie-in material as 'the Land of Fiction', and for convenience's sake this is how it shall be referred to in this book.

a whole tradition of British children's fiction to which the series was an heir.'[9]

This is very true, but much of that debt repayment comes from the way in which Sherwin's story invites us into a separate realm of reality. Lewis, in particular, was fascinated by the ideas of Plato, and his character Digory Kirke specifically cites Plato in *The Last Battle* (1956):

> 'But that was not the real Narnia [...] It was only a shadow or a copy of the real Narnia which has always been here and always will be here: just as our world, England and all, is only a shadow or copy of something in Aslan's real world. [...] And of course it is different; as different as a real thing is from a shadow or as waking life is from a dream. [...] It's all in Plato, all in Plato: bless me, what **do** they teach them at these schools!'[10]

Plato's concept of the world of Forms was of a realm outside the temporal and spatial universe, in which ideas existed, separate from their physical instantiation. In Plato's philosophy (and especially in the developments of it from the Renaissance onwards known as Neoplatonism, which built on Plato's work), everything in the real world is a mere shadow of a perfect, literally idealised, version of itself which exists in this realm. While things in our world are seen to die or decay, in the Platonic realm they are eternal, and free of impurity.

---

[9] Wood, Tat, and Lawrence Miles, *About Time: The Unauthorized Guide to Doctor Who #2 – 1966-1969: Seasons 4 to 6*, (2007), p 217.
[10] Lewis, CS, *The Last Battle* (1956), pp159-60.

This Platonic philosophy influenced, directly or indirectly, almost every major children's author of the early 20th century, and while the fictional characters in *The Mind Robber,* as we shall see, mostly belong to an older tradition, the structure created by Sherwin's additional episode links the story to the Carroll/Nesbit/Lewis tradition of philosophical children's fiction dealing with other worlds that run by other rules – often rules of narrative rather than laws of physics.

For the shooting of the second episode, the programme ran into another problem, which again Sherwin had to solve. Frazer Hines, who played the Doctor's companion Jamie, had come down with chickenpox and so was unavailable to film the episode, in which his character played a necessary part[11]. Sherwin's solution was to have Jamie turned into a cardboard cutout by one of the creatures of the Land of Fiction, and for the Doctor to have to reassemble his face as a puzzle, which he would get wrong, allowing the part to be recast for the episode and part of the subsequent one. Hines filmed the scene of Jamie being turned into the puzzle on his return, and it was edited into the episode, while the part of Jamie was played for a brief time by Hamish Wilson[12].

---

[11] *Doctor Who: The Complete History* #13. *Stories 45-47: The Mind Robber, The Invasion and The Krotons* (2015), p29.
[12] At this point it is obligatory for books of this nature to say something like 'contrary to myth, Hamish Wilson is not Frazer Hines' cousin, although Hines' brother Ian Hines **does** play a soldier in this story.' However, I have never come across this myth myself, only debunkings of it in almost every documentary source on the story. Possibly the myth is itself a myth, which would at least be appropriate given the story under discussion.

Hines' illness falling during this particular story was in many ways a godsend, as in any other story they would have had to rewrite the scripts dramatically, and Jamie's role in the plot would have to be cut or assigned to another character. In this case, though, when dealing with a story in which characters could be magically changed, and which deals with questions of reality and identity, the recasting of Jamie not only made perfect sense but added a much-needed level of tension to the story – the TARDIS crew weren't safe, and could be changed into something different, at any time. The threat in the later episodes of them being turned into fictional characters and losing their identities becomes much more dreadful when one has seen the very identity of Jamie already violated in this way.

After Hines' illness, the production hit few other problems (the most widely-told anecdote simply involves them having to obtain some white paint to make a horse into a convincing unicorn)[13], and progressed relatively smoothly, but these two problems between them turned *The Mind Robber* into something far more sinister, more surreal, and more thought-provoking than the original synopsis suggested.

---

[13] Told in, for instance, Howe, Stammers, Walker, *The Handbook*, p277.

THE THEMES

Appropriately enough for a story with multiple authors, a lot of *The Mind Robber* is fundamentally about the question of authorship, and about to what extent fictional creations can take on a life separate from their creators.

Wood and Miles argue that the main distinction between fantasy and science fiction is that fantasy is about people's relationship with words and symbols, while science fiction is about people's relationship with their physical tools[14]. This definition, like all definitions of the boundary between the two genres, is hopelessly inadequate, but it does capture something of the distinction, certainly if one looks primarily at the kinds of fantasy that have influenced **Doctor Who** in the past – mostly 19th- and early 20th-century children's fiction, rather than the sub-Tolkien material that has formed much of the genre's commercial presence since the 1980s. By this definition, *The Mind Robber* is about as clear-cut an example of fantasy as possible. Things within the Land of Fiction are defined by their nature as words, not as physical objects – a sword can become a dictionary, because 'words' is an anagram of 'sword'[15], and the fictional characters within the Land can have their actions dictated merely by them being written down. The Land of Fiction itself resembles a Platonic realm of Forms, but the Forms here are changeable – they exist outside spacetime, but within narrative, and while they are normally trapped in the roles

---

[14] Wood, Tat, and Lawrence Miles, *About Time: The Unauthorized Guide to Doctor Who #4 – 1975-1979: Seasons 12 to 17*, (2004), pp 129-31.
[15] Episode 2.

to which they are assigned by the narratives in which they first appear, they can be moved into new roles by having their stories rewritten.

Notably, many of the characters we see in the Land are fictionalised versions of real people, behaving as they do in stories created long after the deaths of their originals. If, as Sherwin's additions to the script seem to suggest (although not outright state), we are looking at some sort of realm of ideas rather than a separate physical realm, it's possible that these characters have gone through the same fictionalising process which Zoe and Jamie get put through in this story. In this world, it seems, the idea of Cyrano de Bergerac is not, as Plato would have thought, a changeless, perfected version of the real man, casting a shadow into the real world that gives a distorted and imperfect view of the higher reality. Rather, the Cyrano of the Land is an impermanent, changeable figure, a shadow of the impressions the real man has left on others' imaginations. If the real Cyrano had a normal nose, but a playwright later portrayed him as having a grotesque proboscis, then the Cyrano of this realm will have a huge hooter.

And so the threat of becoming fictional is a threat to the idea of the self, of free will, and of identity. Jamie is changed in appearance at the whim of the Master[16], and when in episode 5 Jamie and Zoe are

---

[16] This character is usually referred to in **Doctor Who** reference works as 'The Master of the Land of Fiction', to distinguish him from the character of the same name who appears regularly from *Terror of the Autons* (1971) onwards. However, the character is only referred to in dialogue or the credits of the serial as 'the

turned into fictional characters, they keep repeating a handful of lines over and again, unable to have any autonomy at all.

When the Doctor is confronted with the plan to fictionalise the whole human race, he is appalled: 'Sausages. Man will just become like a string of sausages, all the same.'[17] Whatever the fictionalising process does, the Doctor believes it removes any individuality from the people who go through it, turning them into little more than the clockwork soldiers we see throughout this story, going through the same motions without any real thought behind them.

(It has to be said, though, that this belief of the Doctor's doesn't appear to stand up when compared with what we see of the Land – the various fictional characters we see all have distinct personalities, with the exception of the toy soldiers, and while they're lacking in free will, they're not the identical 'string of sausages' the Doctor talks about.)

Yet the one writing the story also appears to be trapped. The reason the Doctor has been drawn to the Land is that the Master, the supposed ruler of the Land, is himself in thrall to a computer, the Master Brain. And here we see a theme that recurs throughout season six – a machine intelligence that requires the creativity of a human to function properly. The Master is being mentally controlled by the Master Brain, but the Master Brain needs the Master to write the stories that take place in the Land.

Master', with no modifier, and will be referred to as such within this work.
[17] Episode 5.

A question arises from this when viewing the serial, though it is not addressed directly in the story itself – is the Land of Fiction the source of all fictional ideas, or is it rather a repository for them? That is, is the Master writing stories which will somehow appear in the brains of writers all over the world, or do characters arrive in the Land of Fiction from elsewhere, and is the Master only manipulating forms that have been created by others?

The implication of the Doctor's line 'You can't blow up a fictional character, Zoe', at the end of episode 5, seems to be the latter. It appears that the characters of the Land of Fiction will continue an independent existence without either the Master or the Master Brain. In which case, are they now subject to the whims of the writers who tell their stories on Earth, or are they now given free will, without anyone to script their actions? Or, perhaps, are they now changeless, like the Platonic Forms to which I have compared them previously?

Uniquely for **Doctor Who**, the form, and even the production history, of the story fit these themes. A story with multiple authors features a character who is an author who fictionalises real people – and that character is, as we shall see later, based in part on Ling himself. The Master, like Ling, repurposes others' characters for his own purposes – almost every story choice made by Ling in writing the story is explicitly also a choice made by the Master, within the fiction, as he is writing the fiction itself.

To read this much into the story could seem, perhaps, to be overreaching. After all, what we have here is a piece of Saturday evening children's TV, from a time in **Doctor Who**'s history when, more than at any other point, it was being aimed at a young audience.

Yet *The Mind Robber* is, when watched, this thematically rich. How much of this is intentional on the part of any one of the production team is of course open to question, but what is undeniable is that between Ling's original script, Sherwin's inspired rewrites to cope with production crises, and David Maloney's evocative, surreal direction, these themes have made their way into the finished serial, and have made *The Mind Robber* far more resonant than it has any right to be.

The Mind Robber is, of course, primarily a children's adventure serial, and it cannot bear the weight of the questions it raises – some of which are among the great questions with which Western philosophy has grappled since Plato – but it manages to wear these themes lightly. They don't distort the plot, which is a concise, action-packed adventure, but they are there for the more attentive viewer, and make *The Mind Robber* almost unique among the surviving 1960s **Doctor Who** episodes in its ability to sustain repeated viewings and close readings.

THE STRUCTURE

Whether due to Ling's lack of familiarity with **Doctor Who**, the unusual production circumstances in which the serial was made, or a combination of the two, there are a number of aspects to the structure of *The Mind Robber* that are unique among **Doctor Who** stories.

The grafted-on opening by Sherwin means that the serial effectively has two 'episode 1's – the story proper does not really start until the second episode – and one could even argue that the **plot** doesn't start until near the end of the story. For much of the adventure, this is a picaresque, with the Doctor, Jamie, and Zoe exploring an unfamiliar landscape and the characters within it. We will look later at the similarities between the Doctor and Lemuel Gulliver, but in this story the Doctor has become part of Gulliver's genre – he, like Gulliver, is our representative in a strange place, discovering the rules along with us, and this is enough to carry the narrative without having to have a plot per se.

This is helped by the brief length of the episodes, which at less than 20 minutes were short enough for novelty alone to hold the attention. Some fan sources[18] have suggested that this was because the script had been expanded to five episodes and didn't have enough material for the longer length. In fact, though, the scripts Ling turned in would have lasted the normal 25 minutes, but Sherwin edited them down to 20 at Troughton's request. Troughton believed that the new episode 1, relying as it did solely on the acting talents of the three principals, put too heavy a

---

[18] Notably *TARDIS Data Core*, 'The Mind Robber (TV story)'.

demand on the cast, and to placate him the rest of the episodes were shortened to give the cast a break[19].

The combination of the picaresque structure of the early episodes and the short episode length does, though, mean that when the plot arrives towards the end of episode 4, it feels perfunctory, dashed-off. It's as if someone has told Ling 'Look, this is a **Doctor Who** story – there needs to be some sort of alien invasion and a secret mastermind, so it's science fiction,' and so he's stuck one of each in as an afterthought. It would be tempting to suggest that this was Sherwin's idea – except that all of Sherwin's other contributions actually emphasised the unusual aspects of the story, rather than conforming to an idea of what **Doctor Who** 'should' be.

Possibly Ling merely thought that a **Doctor Who** story had to include something like that, but the result is a rather lop-sided story, with a comparatively leisurely build-up to a rushed climax and a sudden, bathetic, 'then I woke up and it was all a dream... **or was it**?' ending. In particular, the story seems to be building to a big reveal of a force behind the Land, before the whole thread is just dropped.

It's noticeable that the moments and images that stay with people from this story (the white, empty, space; the TARDIS floating in the void; Medusa; the unicorn; Jamie's face changing; the Karkus; the clockwork soldiers) all come from the earlier, plotless, episodes. That the story succeeds so well is a powerful argument in favour of the view of **Doctor Who** that says the plots are secondary to the presentation of unusual images and environments.

---

[19] *The Complete History* #13 p23.

SEASON SIX, EH?

Season six of **Doctor Who** has an unfortunately low reputation among fans, compared to the seasons on either side of it. Season seven is regarded as one of the classics of the series[20], and will always be fondly remembered for introducing the Earth-based UNIT stories that would define Jon Pertwee's time as the Doctor. Meanwhile season five's reputation as being 'the classic monster season' has held up largely despite the quality of the season itself, which is mostly fairly poor, thanks in large part to the fact that until October 2013 only one complete serial from the season survived[21], so its reputation was based on ageing, nostalgic fan memory and novelisations, rather than on the actual broadcast stories.

Season six, on the other hand, had the reputational misfortune to be largely intact. 37 of the season's 44 episodes exist, and the missing episodes are concentrated in only two stories[22], so this season has largely been available for fans to watch and judge on its own merits.

Those merits are plentiful, but they are largely not the kind which **Doctor Who** fandom looks for in the series. There are no introductions of new recurring monsters (the two monsters introduced in this season, the Quarks and the Krotons, are widely regarded as among the series' most ridiculous, and neither has as

---

[20] See for example the introduction to Myles, LM, *The Black Archive #3: The Ambassadors of Death* (2015).
[21] *The Tomb of the Cybermen* (1967). The rediscovery of *The Enemy of the World* (1967-67) was announced on 11 October 2013.
[22] *The Invasion* (1968) and *The Space Pirates* (1969).

yet reappeared in televised **Doctor Who**), the only continuity point established is in the very last episode of the season, with the arrival into the series of the Time Lords, and in general it doesn't keep to the formulae of the seasons on either side.

But surely not keeping to a formula should be a good thing? Well, yes. But it means that season six can't be categorised in the way the seasons around it can, so it's never developed an identity in the fan imagination in the way those seasons have. The stories from season six have to stand or fall on their own merits, rather than as representatives of a 'classic year', and so they tend to get overlooked in discussions of the show[23].

Yet looked at in isolation, the serials in the season, with two possible exceptions, are exceptionally strong. *The Mind Robber,* the focus of this book, is among the best things the series ever did. *The War Games* (1969) manages, astonishingly, to be a tense, thrilling, adventure even when stretched over 10 episodes. *The Krotons* (1968-69) is a strong script, stylishly directed, with only an unfortunate monster costume to let it down. *The Invasion* (1968) is the prototype for everything that the Pertwee era will do, and does it better than many of those later stories will, while *The Seeds of Death* (1969) is a last hurrah for the base-under-siege style, and one of the best examples of its type.

Of the 'two possible exceptions' mentioned earlier, one is impossible to judge. *The Space Pirates* (1969) is almost entirely

---

[23] A similar example might be Graham Williams' first year as producer, season 15, which fell between the two stools of the Hinchcliffe era's horror and the comedy of seasons 16 and 17.

missing from the archives, and while audio recordings of the missing episodes do exist, the story is so slow-paced and visual that it is almost impossible to get any real sense of what the story was like. Should any further episodes of the story be discovered, it may well be re-evaluated by fandom.

The Dominators is another matter. On paper, it shares a lot in common with *The Mind Robber,* but as we will see below, no story could be further from it, either in tone or in quality. It is a very well-known story, and known entirely for its failings.

But leaving *The Dominators* aside for now, what we have in season six is one of the very strongest **Doctor Who** seasons, with one of the strongest sets of regular characters. By this point Troughton and Hines have developed an extraordinary rapport, and while this was Padbury's first and only year in the role, the character of Zoe is strong enough that there was some suggestion of keeping her for the next season (in the scientific assistance role filled by Liz Shaw).

Zoe Herriot (Wendy Padbury)

Zoe is a particularly interesting character, because for the first time (and the only time until season 16) the Doctor is travelling with a companion who is his intellectual equal[24], and who knows more than the viewers at home about the situations in which the TARDIS crew find themselves. This means that there's now an interesting shift in the character of the Doctor. Where previously his role in the story often depended on him solving problems intellectually, and on using scientific knowledge his companions didn't have,

---

[24] Dr Liz Shaw in season seven might be considered the Doctor's intellectual equal, but she doesn't actually travel with him.

increasingly over season six we see him using wisdom, rather than knowledge, to solve problems. The Doctor is no longer defined by his intelligence, but by his experience.

We see this in *The Krotons*, where Zoe solves the intelligence tests faster than the Doctor, but we also see it in a surprising way in *The Mind Robber*, in the fight with the Karkus. Here Zoe is in possession of information – that the Karkus is a fictional character – which the Doctor doesn't have. The Doctor's unfamiliarity with early 21st-century popular culture puts him at the same kind of disadvantage that his companions often find themselves at when confronted with the Doctor's greater knowledge[25].

The character of Zoe had first been introduced in *The Wheel in Space*, the seventh and final story of season five, after the departure of Deborah Watling's character Victoria in the previous story, *Fury From the Deep* (1968). Zoe is a young girl (supposedly in her mid-teens, though Wendy Padbury, the actor playing the character, was much older, and as we will see she is sexualised by the camera in a way which would be deeply disturbing were the viewer to read the character as that young), who has been through

---

[25] It's fun to speculate, to take a Watsonian attitude for a moment, that the Doctor's familiarity with popular entertainment in the 21st-century series stems from this – that his knowledge of **EastEnders** (1985-, referenced by the Doctor in *The Impossible Planet* (2006)) and the **Harry Potter** books (starting with *Harry Potter and the Philosophers' Stone* (1997), and referenced by the Doctor in *The Shakespeare Code* (2007)) is an attempt to compensate for his earlier lack of knowledge of the popular culture of a few decades from now. One wonders if he read back-issues of the *Hourly Telepress* in anticipation of a return match.

a hothousing process designed to create a super-intelligent, super-competent scientist, a 'human computer'.

The name of the character actually came from Ling's 'Manpower' proposal – when Ling was writing, the character had not yet been named, he used 'Zoe' as a placeholder name, and the suggestion was taken up by Sherwin[26].

Padbury had first come to public notice as a member of the cast of **Crossroads** two years earlier, and other than a cameo role in the Albert Finney film vehicle *Charlie Bubbles* (1967), she had had no acting roles of note prior to starting work on **Doctor Who**, though she had a moderately successful career afterwards presenting children's television and appearing in low-budget British films, before going on to become an agent (representing many former **Doctor Who** stars, and towards the end of her career discovering Matt Smith).

Zoe, as played by Padbury, is bright, hugely confident in her own intelligence and knowledge, but much less confident, at least at first, in her social skills and place in her community. If such a character were created today, one suspects she would be coded as having Asperger's syndrome, or otherwise suggested to be a 'geek' in the stereotypical manner. But in 1968, before such stereotypes had become commonplace in popular culture, she was portrayed as being a bubbly, sociable, young woman, eager to please and to impress.

---

[26] Howe, Stammers and Walker, *The Handbook*, p265.

Zoe would remain with the series throughout season six, and unlike many companion characters would actually continue to be characterised as competent and knowledgeable, rather than being reverted to a generic role – while the character screams a lot, and has to be rescued, she also solves many of the problems the TARDIS crew face throughout the season, and is shown to be the Doctor's equal at solving intelligence tests in *The Krotons*, and to be able to program ALGOL off the top of her head well enough to make a computer break down in *The Invasion*. Her knowledge of 21st-century pop culture, and of some form of Judo-like martial arts, also allow her to defeat the Karkus in the present story.

The characterisation of the companions in 20th-century **Doctor Who** has often been criticised, with some justification; but while, like all the companions, Zoe is defined more by the plot role into which she is placed than by a well-rounded, novelistic set of human characteristics, she does at least have character traits which persist between stories, and is far more consistently portrayed than many of the other companions in the series.

The Doctor (Patrick Troughton)

Troughton's Doctor had always been something of a liminal figure – it's not until Pertwee that the Doctor becomes a leading man's part, rather than a part for a character actor (and many would argue that the role lost something then which it has never really recovered) – but over the course of season six he becomes ever more a figure at the edge of the narrative, one who is not so much the protagonist as an antagonist – someone who appears in a previously stable situation, destabilises it, and then disappears before a new status quo can properly be established.

Troughton's Doctor was, for many years, regarded by **Doctor Who** fandom as something of a comical character, thanks to his appearances in the special episodes *The Three Doctors* (1972-73) and *The Five Doctors* (1983), in which he gives almost a caricature of his earlier performances, owing more to fan memory than to anything he did during his original tenure in the role[27]. In fact, though, Troughton's performance is possibly the most subtle and nuanced ever given by an actor in the role.

At this time, the character of the Doctor was fairly well defined, but little was known of his background – he was several centuries old, a traveller in time and space, and we knew of at least one other of his people, the 'Meddling Monk' who had appeared in *The Time Meddler* (1965) and *The Daleks' Master Plan* (1965-66), but other than that the audience knew very little of his background. The words 'Time Lord' had yet to be spoken on the show, and 'Gallifrey' wouldn't be heard of until *The Time Warrior* (1973) was broadcast.

And, of course, prior to Troughton, only one actor had ever played the part in the series[28], so he essentially had to create the part himself, as playing it in the same way as Hartnell wasn't really an option. Troughton's portrayal, far more than Hartnell's, has become the one which other actors look to as the default

---

[27] Troughton also returned to the role in *The Two Doctors* (1985), but this performance was rather less of a caricature.

[28] Not counting, of course, stand-ins and body doubles. Peter Cushing had also played the role, in *Doctor Who and the Daleks* (1965) and *Daleks: Invasion Earth 2150 AD* (1966), and would have been another point of comparison.

characterisation for the Doctor, a template for them to adhere to or vary from, but always knowing that that is what they are doing.

In *The Mind Robber*, the Doctor is fleshed out rather more than he had been previously, thanks to the peculiar nature of the story – for once we get to discover something of the Doctor's interests, as we learn his love of *Gulliver's Travels* (1726, corrected edition 1735), a book from which he can recite large chunks from memory. We also get to see that he has a rather greater horror for the idea of his companions becoming fictional, and thus losing their free will, than he normally has for more physical dangers. The nature of the Doctor as a character can never really change, because of the style and genre of the narrative in which he is embedded, but *The Mind Robber*, more than most of Troughton's stories, at least elaborates on that nature to a small extent, because for once it's a story about the mind, and a mental threat, rather than the external threats which Troughton's Doctor normally faces.

Jamie McCrimmon (Frazer Hines and Hamish Wilson)

Jamie McCrimmon, the third member of the TARDIS crew for season six, appears in all but one of Troughton's stories as the Doctor[29]. He joined it at the end of *The Highlanders* (1966-67), Troughton's second story in the role, and would remain until the last episode of *The War Games*, Troughton's last regular appearance in the show.

---

[29] Not counting *The Three Doctors*, made three years after the end of Troughton's tenure as the Doctor. The other two stories which feature Troughton returning to the role, *The Five Doctors* and *The Two Doctors,* do however feature the character.

Jamie is an 18th-century Highland soldier, although as with many of the companions in the 1960s his background is only alluded to infrequently, usually with a single line in a story in which he is mystified by some piece of common 20th-century technology such as an aeroplane. He is ferociously loyal to the Doctor, even though he often mistrusts or doubts him, and he is prone to understanding complex concepts in simple metaphorical terms (which of course allows those concepts to be explained to the younger children watching the show, who might otherwise not themselves have been able to follow the plot).

So Jamie fulfils multiple different plot functions. He's there to take on the action hero role previously filled by Ian, Steven and Ben, but also to be the young person to whom the plot can be explained – the role that many female companions, before and since, have played. This is especially the case once Zoe comes on board, as Zoe by her nature is not a character who needs to have concepts like computers explained to her, and indeed is likely to be the one doing the explaining.

In *The Mind Robber*, due to Hines' chickenpox, Jamie is played for two episodes, for the first and only time, by someone other than Hines – the Scottish actor Hamish Wilson, who manages to do a remarkably good job of matching Hines' performance (though not, understandably, his voice or accent, Wilson keeping his own accent rather than Hines' stage Scots) – convincing us that the character is still the same, even though his face has changed.

Peter Ling

Peter Ling, the writer of *The Mind Robber*, was best known at the time for having co-created **Crossroads**, a soap opera[30] set in a motel near Birmingham, for the ITV network.

However, Ling's pre-soap career is rather more relevant to *The Mind Robber*[31]. He had written for the first ever children's TV series, **Whirligig** (1950-56), scripting the adventures of Mr Turnip, a puppet voiced by Peter Hawkins, before moving to Associated-Rediffusion TV, where he script-edited their children's programming. He'd also written, with his wife Sheilah Ward, several episodes of **The Avengers** (1961-69), and so was aware of the demands both of action serials and of children's TV. So while he was not keen on the science fiction or fantasy genres (and indeed never wrote in either again), he understood the conventions of the other genres which **Doctor Who** had to straddle well enough that he was a relatively safe pair of hands.

---

[30] The term 'soap opera' means something rather different in Britain to its meaning in the USA. British soap operas are, like their American counterparts, ongoing serialised dramas, but there the resemblances end. Modern mainstream soap operas in the UK deal almost exclusively with working-class life, usually in poorer areas of provincial cities like Manchester, Liverpool, or, in the case of **Crossroads**, Birmingham. The sort of glamorous life portrayed in American soap operas is completely alien to the British genre.

[31] All biographical details of Ling come from his obituary in *The Independent* (Hayward, Anthony, 'Peter Ling', *The Independent*, 26 September 2006).

Derrick Sherwin

Derrick Sherwin was the script editor of **Doctor Who** for much of seasons five and six, as well as being producer for the final story of season six. Sherwin also wrote, uncredited, the first episode of *The Mind Robber*, having already written the last episode of *The Dominators*.

Sherwin is a rather overlooked figure in the history of **Doctor Who**, but he introduced many of the concepts which have come to be most associated with the series. Sherwin was largely or wholly responsible for, among other aspects of the series, the sonic screwdriver, UNIT, and the Time Lords.

Sherwin's main desire when working on **Doctor Who** was to take the formula that had been developed over the previous couple of seasons and scrap it. Sherwin thought that alien monsters of the type that were regularly turning up at bases throughout the solar system and menacing small multi-ethnic groups were laughable, and he wanted to make the series more like the **Quatermass** serials (1953-59)[32], a series which he thought was one of the few examples of science fiction working really well on television.

What he wanted to do was to ground the series in reality, and to take away the aspects that seemed to him ridiculous – to make

---

[32] Possibly the most influential British science fiction series of all time, a series of short serials written by Nigel Kneale involving a scientist working with the 'British Rocket Group' and investigating alien incursions. **Quatermass** has been cited as an influence by generations of television writers.

people want to tune in for reasons other than merely to see what kind of monster costume would be used that week.

To quote Sherwin:

> 'I think people get bored with seeing monsters all the time. They get bored with seeing funny planets and weird frogs and people with trees growing out of their ears. Going back into history, as well – the historical bits were incredibly boring [...] I personally felt that at that time it was absolutely essential to bring it down to Earth, to get the audience back...'[33]

However, while Sherwin thought the monsters were getting boring, he was clearly not averse to strangeness per se, as he commissioned *The Mind Robber* as the final story of his main run as script editor (he returned briefly as script editor for *The Space Pirates* as Terrance Dicks, his successor, was working on writing the scripts for *The War Games*).

Peter Bryant

Peter Bryant, the producer of almost all of season six and half of season five of **Doctor Who**, would be at first glance the last person one would expect to produce a story as outlandish as *The Mind Robber*. Bryant's own instincts were always to go for 'realistic' stories with plots set on Earth and minimal fantastic elements, in order to ground the story – while he didn't coin the term, he is as responsible as anyone for the 'Yeti in the loo' type of story which characterised Jon Pertwee's tenure in the role. He was as keen as

---

[33] Howe, Stammers and Walker, *The Handbook*, p241.

Derrick Sherwin to move away from the base-under-siege stories that characterised the series when he came on to it, and indeed it is very difficult to separate the two men's influence, as both seem (at least in retrospective interviews) to have had very similar visions for the series.

Bryant believed that children responded better to stories set in familiar locations:

> 'They'd know if a story was in the London Underground, because they'd know what an Underground station looks like [...] I just thought "Let's get back down on Earth again. Let's get somewhere the kids can identify with the actors, with the characters".'[34]

He and Sherwin worked out the new format for the series, which would start with *Spearhead from Space* (1970), and which would involve the Doctor being a scientific advisor to the military on contemporary Earth.

However, despite Bryant's own preference for 'realistic' stories based on contemporary Earth, he was flexible enough to commission and produce a season in which only one story takes place in familiar terrestrial surroundings.

Bryant and Sherwin's working relationship continued past **Doctor Who**, as when Bryant became producer of **Paul Temple** (1969-71), he persuaded Sherwin, who succeeded him as **Doctor Who** producer, to join him as script editor on the second season.

---

[34] Howe, Stammers, Walker, *The Handbook*, p241.

David Maloney

David Maloney, the director of *The Mind Robber,* is in many ways the most prominent creative figure in **Doctor Who**'s sixth season, directing 19 of its 44 episodes, including the 10-part closing story *The War Games*. When Maloney directed *The Mind Robber*, it was his first time directing **Doctor Who**, and one of his very earliest directorial jobs (though not, as sometimes reported, his first – he had directed two episodes of **Z Cars** (1962-78) and one of **The Newcomers** (1965-69) before *The Mind Robber*), but it shows the visual imagination that would characterise Maloney's work throughout his time on the series.

Most of the series' directors were competent, workmanlike people who got the job done but were far from being auteurs. Only a handful of directors during the first 26 years of the series managed to combine the ability to work with actors, a strong storytelling instinct, and a strong visual imagination. Arguably only three – Maloney, Douglas Camfield, and Graeme Harper – did so well enough, and with enough individuality, that one can identify their work without knowing in advance that they were the director[35].

All of Maloney's stories, with the possible exception of the rather poor *Planet of the Daleks* (1973), share a characteristic sense of Gothic horror and surrealism[36]. The stories Maloney directed often

---

[35] One can identify the work of Barry Letts, too, but while he had an identifiable directorial style, he was not an especially good director, being merely solid in most people's estimation.

[36] They are *The Mind Robber, The Krotons, The War Games, Planet of the Daleks, Genesis of the Daleks* (1975), *Planet of Evil* (1975), *The Deadly Assassin* (1976) and *The Talons of Weng-Chiang* (1977).

feature some sort of artificial or constructed reality, or a sense that there is a truth that is hidden from view – something that is certainly true of *The Mind Robber*. They're also often set in places where the very landscape itself is malevolent, sometimes subject to control by others – Maloney's work has a strong sense of place, and many of the spaces his shots create give the impression that the very geography and weather are out to harm the heroes. The result is a sense of creeping paranoia, as the world created by Maloney's direction slowly gives up its secrets and is revealed to be far more hostile than it initially appears.

Maloney also often casts the same actors in multiple stories (Philip Madoc, Bernard Horsfall and Michael Wisher to give three prominent examples), and this adds to the sense of him as an auteur in a way that few other **Doctor Who** directors can claim to be. While some of Maloney's more distinctive visual motifs (such as the repeated use of gas-masks in his stories) have not yet appeared as of *The Mind Robber*, it is clearly of a piece with his later work, and instantly recognisable as by the same director as those later stories.

The Other Stories in Season Six

It's worth looking, briefly, at the other stories that were produced for *Doctor Who's* sixth season, in order to see to what extent there was an overall aesthetic vision for the season itself, and whether *The Mind Robber* fitted that vision or was an aberration. Here we're looking at the season as broadcast, from *The Dominators* to *The War Games*, but it is important to remember that *The Dominators* and *The Mind Robber* were made by a rather different team than the later stories (though the last two years of

Troughton's tenure in the role can best be described as a production team game of musical chairs, with people regularly taking over each other's jobs as circumstances demanded).

The gaps between seasons in the 1960s were not as important as in later decades, as the series was on almost all year round – indeed, while there was a 10-week gap between seasons five and six, seven weeks of that gap were taken up with a repeat of the season four serial *The Evil of the Daleks* (1967) (introduced in-story at the end of *The Wheel in Space* by the Doctor telling Zoe he was going to show her 'the sort of thing that she may be in for'[37], the only time a repeat has ever been included like this in the story's narrative). So there were only three weeks between 2 September 1967 (the start of season five) and 21 June 1969 (the end of season six, with the last episode of *The War Games*) when **Doctor Who** wasn't on the air.

This means that *The Dominators* would not have been seen as a 'season premiere' or jumping-on point, any more than *The Wheel in Space* would have been seen as a 'season finale' in the contemporary sense. They were episodes in an ongoing serial which took occasional short breaks, rather than in a short season of a show which wouldn't come back for nearly a year, as in later years.

However, it's still true that it makes sense to talk of 'season five' and 'season six' as discrete bodies of work. Season five's focus on monsters is almost completely gone by season six, where the monsters still exist in most stories, but are almost incidental to the

---

[37] *The Wheel in Space*, episode 6.

plots. The Cybermen, for example, don't appear until the fourth episode of the eight-episode *The Invasion*. Season six also features several new creative forces, notably Maloney and Robert Holmes, who give the series a more mature, sophisticated feeling than the earlier season.

The Dominators

At first glance, *The Dominators* has a lot in common with *The Mind Robber*. Both are stories made at the end of the recording block that had started with *The Abominable Snowmen*, the second story of season five. Both stories are five episodes long, rather than the more usual four or six. Both feature unusual writing credits, with *The Mind Robber*'s first episode being the only one in the programme's history to be broadcast without a writing credit[38], while *The Dominators* is credited to 'Norman Ashby', a pseudonym combining the names of the fathers-in-law of the story's principal writers[39], Henry Lincoln and Mervyn Haisman. These writers had asked for their names to be removed from *The Dominators* as broadcast, because it was so different from their own conception.

---

[38] That we know of. As ever, it is difficult to make generalisations about the series without acknowledging that 97 (at last count as of this writing) of the 1960s episodes are missing. Given that incorrect credits went out on occasion, we can't rule out the possibility of there having been other Hartnell or Troughton stories which went out without a writing credit. It is, however, definitely the only episode to go out with the writer's name **deliberately** missing.

[39] I say 'principal' writers, as the script transmitted was apparently very different from the one submitted.

The Dominators is a poor attempt at social satire, but even as poor as it is, it's still noticeable that it's not a typical base-under-siege story, and that it attempts to create a whole alien society for the Doctor to visit, rather than having the only aliens be a group of generic monsters. This is, of course, rather countered by the fact that the antagonists actually call themselves 'the Dominators'[40], about the most generic-monster name it is possible to imagine, short of calling themselves 'the Baddies'.

The story was originally intended to be six episodes long, but because of the poor quality of the story, it was cut down by an episode, with Sherwin largely writing the fourth episode with his assistant Terrance Dicks[41], and the fifth and sixth episodes of the script being combined into a single final episode. Even as it is, it feels padded, and is the one definite failure of the season.

The Invasion

An eight-part story involving a Cyberman invasion of the Earth, this story was intended as a way of testing a new format for **Doctor Who**, in which rather than travel through space and time as before, the Doctor would be based on Earth and providing scientific support to a military organisation dedicated to dealing with the unusual and alien.

---

[40] A name which, to this writer at least, only adds to the bathetic effect of the story as a whole by calling to mind Peter Cook's EL Wisty and his World Domination League (*Peter Cook Presents The Misty Mr Wisty*, 1965).
[41] Wood and Miles, *About Time #2*, p209.

The result is probably the most accurate idea we can get of what Sherwin and Bryant's vision for the series was. And it has to be said that if Sherwin and Bryant's ideas had been realised as well as they were in this story, they would have made a quite excellent series – but one which, fundamentally, had little to do with **Doctor Who** as it has been for much of its run.

To the extent that *The Invasion* is about anything at all (other than Cybermen, action sequences, and stock footage), it's about the balance between logic and emotion, humanity and machinery. The plot is based around the attempts by the evil industrialist Tobias Vaughan, head of International Electromatics, to help his alien allies, the Cybermen, take over the world. For much of the story, the focus is on Vaughan and his interactions with the TARDIS crew. It becomes apparent, however, that Vaughan is only part human, and has been partly converted into a Cyberman himself. But Vaughan is working on both sides – as well as plotting with the Cybermen to take over Earth, he has also been working on a machine, the cerebratron mentor, which will induce emotion in the Cybermen and kill them, in case they decide to betray him.

This makes for an interesting parallel with a scene in episode 2, in which Zoe manages to disable one of International Electromatics' computers, by giving it an insoluble logic problem, causing it to explode. We see here a recurring theme which we also see in *The Mind Robber* – logic on its own is deadly, but so too is too much emotion. Only human creativity can combine the two in the 'correct' proportions.

The Krotons

The second story directed by David Maloney, *The Krotons*, is a four-part story (the only four-part story of the season, and one of only two surviving four-part stories that Troughton appeared in), the first **Doctor Who** serial to be written by Robert Holmes.

Much like *The Dominators*, *The Krotons* is an attempt to show a truly alien society at work while commenting on the political situation of the time (it even has rioting students) yet unlike *The Dominators* it largely works, apart from some poor monster designs, thanks to a combination of Robert Holmes' witty script and Maloney's direction.

The Krotons is, in essence, a reworking of the myth of Theseus and the Minotaur (a myth which, of course, is referenced in *The Mind Robber* itself), with the two brightest Gonds (the race of humanoids in the story) taken to be 'companions' of the villainous Krotons each year and having their brains drained.

Again we see a machine intelligence seeking humanoids for their problem-solving abilities (as the Doctor is sought in *The Mind Robber*) but being defeated when that problem-solving ability is turned against them.

The Seeds of Death

A six-part story involving the return of the Ice Warriors, popular villains who had appeared in the previous season's base-under-siege story *The Ice Warriors* (1967).

While the story is a return to the base-under-siege formula, after months of experimentation it feels, in context, rather different. Season six has been, in large part, about trying different approaches to the series – hallucinatory fantasy, satire, military conspiracy thriller – to see which ones are useful approaches for the future. As part of that strategy, it feels like there is almost an obligation to try the season five formula as well, to see if that can be made to work.

And it does work. In a season which seems to be saying '**Doctor Who** can do **this**, and **this**, and **this**', it shows that one of the things it can do is the stuff it's done in the past, and that there is still life in the old formulae, in moderation.

The Space Pirates

This six-part story is largely missing from the archives, which is a shame as it seems to have been a uniquely visual story. It doesn't sound like it will have been terribly impressive, but without more information it's more or less impossible even to talk sensibly about.

The War Games

The last story of season six is also the last story of the black-and-white era of *Doctor Who*, and the last story to feature Troughton, Hines, or Padbury as regular cast members. It also features the **Doctor Who** writing debut of two more **Crossroads** writers – Terrance Dicks (who had been script editor for much of the season, taking over from Sherwin, whose assistant he had previously been) and Malcolm Hulke. Dicks and Hulke would go on to be two of the most important creative forces in **Doctor Who** for the next several years; Dicks as script editor for the whole of Jon Pertwee's five years in the role (and writer of several major stories for Tom Baker and one for Peter Davison), Hulke as writer of several of the most well-regarded stories during Pertwee's run.

Other than *The Daleks' Master Plan*, which is something of a special case, *The War Games* is the longest *Doctor Who* story ever[42], lasting a whole 10 episodes, and it had a scale to match its length. The story appears at first to be set in the trenches of the First World War, but slowly the full scale of the story is revealed, as we see the alien War Lords have taken human soldiers from throughout Earth's history and set them against each other.

The War Games is directed by Maloney, and again deals with the themes of hidden realities and unseen manipulators that characterise so many of his stories. Maloney contributed many ideas during the planning stages of the story, which seems very much to have been written to his strengths.

In particular, much like *The Mind Robber*, it combines characters and situations of very different origins, in an almost collage-like approach to building a story. While many *Doctor Who* stories feature the collision of different characters and genres – indeed the series is almost a machine for creating such collisions – rarely has it done so to the extent that happens in *The War Games* and *The Mind Robber*. This is very much a hallmark of Maloney's work on the series – he creates similar bricolage-style juxtapositions in the opening scenes of *Genesis of the Daleks* (1975), in episode three of

---

[42] *The Trial of a Time Lord* (1986) doesn't really count in this case, being three separate, shorter stories with a framing sequence and a two-part epilogue. Given that the trial plot barely impinges at all on most of the action, it's fair to consider this more like the story arcs we see in the series from 2005 on, with plot threads dropped in otherwise standalone stories coming together in a two-part season finale.

The Deadly Assassin (1976), and to a lesser extent in *The Talons of Weng-Chiang* (1977).

And so having looked at season six we can see patterns emerging. Reality is not what it seems, and is being manipulated by powerful figures. The apparent villains themselves are being manipulated too, often by machine intelligences, and computers are not to be trusted. Computers and other machines need human or humanoid emotion and creativity in order to get past the limits of their own logic. And these recurring themes are dealt with in as many different styles as it is reasonably possible for a family adventure series to do. The show is casting around for new directions and new formats in which to tell its stories, but the production team have a very clear idea of what kind of stories they want to tell in those new formats.

There is no typical season six story – the stories this season vary more than almost any other in terms of length, structure, and indeed quality – but precisely because of that, an atypical story like *The Mind Robber* fits in as well as anything else.

THE CHARACTERS OF THE LAND OF FICTION

Perhaps surprisingly, the Land of Fiction's inhabitants, at least as seen on screen, include relatively few established fictional characters. In a land based on fiction, one would expect to see many familiar characters from novels and stories, perhaps something along the lines of **The League of Extraordinary Gentlemen** (1999-), with its cast of Victorian pulp-adventure heroes[43].

Yet other than the central cast, the characters in the serial are an odd mix of newly-invented characters, non-speaking monsters of myth, and fictionalised versions of real people, with Lancelot, Rapunzel, and Gulliver being the only human characters to have their origins clearly in non-**Doctor Who** fiction.

In some cases, this is because characters Ling wished to use in his initial drafts proved to be unavailable for copyright reasons (notably Zorro was removed from an early version of the scripts because of these concerns[44]), and some characters are clearly intended to stand in for more well-known figures. Yet it is curious how almost all of them are figures that straddle the borderline between fiction and reality.

---

[43] Indeed comic writer Scott Gray took this approach in 'Character Assassin', a comic strip in *Doctor Who Magazine* #311, in which the Master (the Gallifreyan opponent of the Doctor, not the character of the same name from *The Mind Robber*) journeys to the Land of Fiction to attend a meeting of villains such as Moriarty and Dracula.
[44] Howe, Stammers and Walker, *The Handbook*, p267.

All the characters chosen, even for the tiniest roles in the story, seem to fit both with the themes of the story and with each other. One gets the impression that Ling and Sherwin paid a great deal of attention to the choices they made – all the characters are ones that would be familiar not only from their fictional sources but from film or television adaptations, so even the less bookish children in the audience would have some idea of their origins. But at the same time, all of these characters seem to be from works which question the boundaries between the real and the fictional, and the concept of an omniscient author separate from the work.

Gulliver (Bernard Horsfall)

Lemuel Gulliver is the protagonist of one of the great novels of the 18th century, and a prime example of this borderline-straddling. *Travels into Several Remote Nations of the World, in Four Parts: By Lemuel Gulliver, First a Surgeon, and then a Captain of Several Ships* (1735) (referred to from now on as *Gulliver's Travels*), by Jonathan Swift, is a work in which the very notion of authorship is questionable.[45]

It's a work that started as part of a group project, which was released pseudonymously, with the publisher being unaware of the author's identity. The book itself makes frequent reference to its own supposed nature as a non-fiction memoir, with Gulliver saying:

> 'If the Censure of Yahoos could any Way affect me, I should have great reason to complain, that some of them are so

---

[45] Much of the argument that follows is indebted to 'Jonathan Swift and *Gulliver's Travels*' by Abigail Williams and Kate O'Connor.

bold as to think my Book of Travels a meer Fiction out of Mine own Brain.'[46]

The manuscript that Swift submitted to publisher Benjamin Motte contained a letter signed by Gulliver's fictional cousin, Richard Sympson, who 'wrote' the introduction to the book, asking for it to be published.

And the authorship of the book got blurred further. The book itself, when first released, differed strongly from the manuscript that Swift submitted. Without the ability to contact the unknown author, Motte took it upon himself to excise and rewrite the more inflammatory portions of the book, much to Swift's displeasure.

So the book presented itself, not as the work of its actual author (who anyway was not the author of the whole book), but rather as the work of its own fictional character. This was a common practice among the travelogue stories which were among Swift's many satirical targets.

And this relationship to the travelogue means that Gulliver is, in a way, one of the Doctor's ancestors, because *Gulliver's Travels* is, in many ways, a very early example of the science fiction genre. Adam Roberts argues that science fiction developed from a variety of different genres: 'fantastic voyage, utopia, future-tale, satire, and so on'[47]. *Gulliver's Travels* has elements of all of the genres in Roberts' incomplete list, with the possible exception of the 'future-tale', and it also engages with and critiques the practice of science itself.

---

[46] Swift, *Gulliver's Travels* (1735), piv.
[47] Roberts, Adam, *The History of Science Fiction* (2005), p4.

Orwell argues that Swift's work is largely directed against science and intellectual curiosity, and that:

> 'he will not allow the scientist — either the 'pure' scientist or the ad hoc investigator — to be a useful person in his own line. Even if he had not written Part III of Gulliver's Travels, one could infer from the rest of the book that, like Tolstoy and like Blake, he hates the very idea of studying the processes of Nature.'[48]

Roberts, however, argues that Swift is engaged in a more nuanced discussion of the potential of science to affect the real world:

> 'The science in this 18th-century science fiction is the science of ocean navigation that enabled Swift's contemporaries to travel to places practically further away and less well-known than was effectively the case for those 1960s Americans who travelled to the Moon.'

He points out that even the most fantastic elements of the voyages are rationalised in terms that are superficially plausible by 18th-century standards — the flying island of the Laputans being kept afloat by a 'loadstone' which is repelled by the ground below, for example.

Roberts argues that:

> 'it needs to be stressed that not only is Swift's great novel **inherently** science-fictional, all four parts are deeply steeped in science, and to such a degree that it becomes hard to avoid reading the book as being **about** science, or more

---

[48] Orwell, George, *Essays*, pp1093-94.

particularly about the relationship between science and representation. Which latter phrase might function, we might think, as a shorthand definition of science fiction itself.'[49]

So Gulliver was the protagonist of a novel which we can take as being one of the first works in the genre to which **Doctor Who** belongs[50].

Gulliver is also, within the fiction to which he belongs, an author – the role for which the Doctor is being groomed by the Master in this story. And more importantly, he is a traveller to strange and exotic new worlds which comment on the world in which his readers lived. In particular, his journeys to Brobdignag and Lilliput are precisely the same kind of experiment with scale as 'sideways' stories from the Hartnell era such as *Planet of Giants* (or, to a lesser extent, *The Web Planet* (1965)).

Gulliver is also, at least at the start of his journeys, a rational, problem-solving, Enlightenment man[51]. He is, in short, if not a

---

[49] Roberts, *The History of Science Fiction*, pp69-72.

[50] While there is some debate as to the extent to which **Doctor Who** counts as 'science fiction', it's fair to say that the series is perceived by most viewers as belonging to that genre, and that any definition of science fiction broad enough to contain *Gulliver's Travels* is also broad enough to contain **Doctor Who**.

[51] Of course, one of the points of Swift's novel was to show what he perceived as the limitations of this kind of thinking, but in the bowdlerised versions of the early sections of the novel, which would have been how most viewers of the serial would have encountered the character, he is much more unambiguously an heroic figure.

prototype of the Doctor, certainly a figure with many similarities to him.

Certainly Ling thought so, saying that the inclusion of Gulliver came 'from my vague thought that Gulliver was a traveller outside the boundaries of space and time.'[52]

However, the character in *The Mind Robber* is also interesting in that of all the fictional characters we meet in the Land of Fiction, he is the only one whose creation can be tied to a single work by a named author, rather than being a fictionalised real person, a character from folk tale, or a newly-created stand-in for a character that was in copyright.

For this reason, Gulliver is the only character who uses a gimmick that Sherwin had suggested – he speaks only in the words that Swift gives Gulliver to speak in the book. Until the narrative starts to break down in the latter stages of the serial, as the Master's grip on the Land starts to weaken, Gulliver is given dialogue that, while appropriate to the situation, comes directly from Swift's novel. Unlike the other characters, Gulliver is defined solely by his author.

Gulliver is played by Bernard Horsfall, who would be cast again by Maloney in three further serials: *The War Games, Planet of the Daleks,* and *The Deadly Assassin* (1976). In two of these three, he plays a member of the Doctor's own race, the Time Lords, and in every story except *Planet* he is positioned as in some way parallel to the Doctor, but morally ambiguous or actively evil. *The Mind Robber* is no exception – while Gulliver does eventually come round

---

[52] Howe, Stammers and Walker, *The Handbook*, p267.

to the Doctor's side, he's positioned at least at first as being antagonistic, and until his identity is revealed the character is coded as suspicious.

The Children (Barbara Loft, Sylvestra Le Tozel, Timothy Horton, Christopher Reynalds, David Reynalds, and Martin Langley)

The children in the serial are not named, but are based on the Bastable children from Edith Nesbit's book *The Treasure Seekers*[53] (1899)[54] and its sequels. In an earlier work, the current author mistakenly (and embarrassingly) claimed that the characters were based on those from Nesbit's more well-known work *The Railway Children* (1906)[55], but while this was incorrect, it seems likely that the idea of using Nesbit characters was inspired by the then-recent TV adaptation of that book, which was a hit when filming started on the serial. The children were a late addition to the story, added in by Derrick Sherwin (Ling's original storyline had their plot function taken by 'brain creatures', who were later revised into the

---

[53] According to, among others, Cornell, Paul, Keith Topping and Martin Day, *Doctor Who: The Discontinuity Guide* (1995), pp92-93, who say the sequence is 'largely drawn from E Nesbit's *Treasure Seekers*'. *The Complete History* quotes the script as describing the children as 'like an E Nesbit illustration' (p19).

[54] The full title of which is actually *The Story of the Treasure Seekers: Being the Adventures of the Bastable Children in Search of a Fortune*.

[55] Hickey, Andrew, *Fifty Stories for Fifty Years: An Unauthorised Guide to the Highlights of Doctor Who* (2013), p39. Similarly, Wood and Miles (*About Time* #2, p216) claim that the children are those from *Five Children and It* (1902), yet another Nesbit work about a group of young children.

toy soldiers who appear elsewhere in the story), and it is hard to imagine Sherwin **not** considering this successful series when making his changes[56].

The characters are not named, as Nesbit's work was still in copyright at the time, but it's interesting to note that *The Treasure Seekers* is another work, like *Gulliver's Travels*, with an unreliable narrator – Oswald, the child who narrates the book, says at the beginning that he won't say until the end which of the children is the narrator, so that 'While the story is going on you may be trying to guess, only I bet you don't'. However, he gives himself away long before the end of the book, 'inadvertently' using the first person.

The Treasure Seekers is also a strong influence on at least one of the strands of children's literature that led to **Doctor Who**. While the influence of the Narnia books on the series is overstated, and mostly seems to amount to a box containing something larger than itself, along with the coincidence of CS Lewis dying the day before **Doctor Who** first aired, the tradition to which they belonged was a definite influence, and Nesbit was one of the progenitors of that tradition – something to which Lewis alluded in the first chapter of *The Magician's Nephew* (1955), where he wrote:

> 'In those days Mr Sherlock Holmes was still living in Baker Street and the Bastables were looking for treasure in the Lewisham Road.'[57]

---

[56] It is perhaps interesting to note that the 1957 TV adaptation of that story had featured, in the role of Roberta (the role famously played by Jenny Agutter in both the 1968 TV version and the later film version), Anneke Willys, who as Anneke Wills had played Polly in **Doctor Who** in 1966 and 1967.

The character of Oswald Bastable would, three years after *The Mind Robber*, be reimagined by Michael Moorcock for a series of novels set in alternative realities, written as a critique of Nesbit's implicit politics (Nesbit was a Fabian socialist)[58].

The Treasure Seekers itself was the first of Nesbit's children's books, and in many ways a prototype for the formula she would follow in all her later stories. It features a group of six children, the Bastables, from an upper-middle-class family that has fallen on hard times, trying to find treasure in order to restore the family's fortune. It has been argued that the story is intended as a satirical argument against capitalism:

> 'In fact, the more traditional and capitalistic their approach, the more trouble the Bastables get into. The lesson is fairly clear: investment, capital speculation, and hard work get you into trouble. (Although, to be fair, hard work, not as much.) Sharing your assets brings rewards.'[59]

However, the popularity of the book with young children, who were not particularly interested in joining the Fabian Society and campaigning for a reforming, democratic socialism, led to Nesbit

---

[57] Lewis, CS, *The Magician's Nephew* (1955), p9. For more on the influence Nesbit had on Lewis, see Nicholson, Mervyn, 'CS Lewis and the Scholarship of Imagination in E Nesbit and Rider Haggard'.

[58] Moorcock, Michael, *Warlord of the Air* (1971), *The Land Leviathan* (1974) and *The Steel Tsar* (1981). Collected in *A Nomad of the Time Streams* (1996).

[59] Ness, Mari, 'Fighting Capitalism Through Children: The Story of the Treasure-Seekers' (2011).

writing many more stories featuring similar groups of children – as Gore Vidal describes it:

> 'Nesbit's usual device is to take a family of children ranging in age from a baby to a child of 10 or 11 and then involve them in adventures, either magical or realistic (never both at the same time).'[60]

These magical adventures often involved a time-travel element (Nesbit may well be the earliest author to write stories of time-travel aimed at children, rather than adults), or a journey to another, separate, world, and Nesbit's influence on the British children's literature of the first half of the 20th century is such that one has to see these stories as distant ancestors of **Doctor Who**. Having the Bastables, in anonymous form, appear in *The Mind Robber* feels like an appropriate acknowledgement.

Rapunzel (Christine Pirie)

Rapunzel is rather an odd one out here, as the only character from European folk stories, and also the only named female non-regular character in a speaking role. The story of Rapunzel, in the form by which it would be best known to children of the 1960s, was collected by the Grimm brothers in 1812, though versions of the story date back (as does so much in *The Mind Robber*, oddly enough) to the 17th century, and to France, in particular to a story by Giambattista Basile called 'Petrosinella', from 1634. (Both Petrosinella and Rapunzel are names, in French and German respectively, of types of leafy vegetable).

---

[60] Vidal, Gore, 'The Writing of E Nesbit', *The New York Review of Books*, 3 December 1964.

The story is much the same in all its variants – a pregnant woman craves a particular vegetable, and so her husband goes and steals some from the garden of a witch, who is understandably annoyed that her vegetables are being stolen, but requires a fine which many would consider excessive – she demands the baby be given to her as soon as it is born.

The baby, named Rapunzel, is brought up by the witch and, when she turns 12, locked into a tower with no door – the only way the witch can enter the tower is to get Rapunzel to let down her golden hair, which the witch can climb to gain entry. This arrangement is disrupted, however, when a passing prince hears the witch calling to Rapunzel and decides to do the same. The witch discovers the relationship between the prince and Rapunzel, but after various travails (which vary depending on the version, and how much sex and violence the authors believe the target audience can cope with) the prince and Rapunzel are united and married.

Sadly, Rapunzel is the only named female character in *The Mind Robber* other than Zoe and Medusa, and none of the three ever exchange any dialogue, thus making this story conclusively fail the 'Bechdel test'[61]. Her role in *The Mind Robber* is minimal, despite

---

[61] The cartoonist Alison Bechdel, in her *Dykes to Watch Out For* (1983-2008), had a character say 'I only go to see a movie if it satisfies three basic requirements. **One**, it has to have at least two women in it, who two, **talk** to each other about, three, something besides a **man**.' Many people have subsequently adopted this as a test which can be applied to films and other works of fiction, usually with the extra proviso that the two female characters be named. The test, as a test, has been widely and accurately criticised, including by Bechdel herself, but is useful as a loose

being one of a tiny number of speaking characters, with most of her actions being just to act as a ladder that happens to be able to speak.

The Minotaur

The Minotaur is the first figure we meet from Greek myth. The Minotaur was, according to legend, a man with the head of a bull, born from an act of copulation between Pasiphaë, Queen of Crete, and a bull[62].

The Minotaur was placed at the centre of a labyrinth, designed by Daedalus, in order to prevent it from escaping, but as it was an unnatural creature, it could only live by eating human beings. Because of this, regular lotteries were drawn and 14 Athenians (seven of each sex[63]) were sent on a regular basis (either every one, seven, or nine years, depending on the source) to Crete to be sent into the labyrinth. Once in the labyrinth, they were expected to be unable to find their way out and to be hunted down by the Minotaur, at least until the hero Theseus decided to secrete a sword and thread about his person – the sword to kill the Minotaur, and the thread to trace his way back to the start of the labyrinth.

---

lower bound for gender representation. Sadly, **Doctor Who** fails the test far more often than is necessary.

[62] This appears to have been a reference to a symbolic 'mystic marriage' between women and bulls, a feature of Minoan religion which the Greeks didn't understand.

[63] The current author does not endorse the ancient Greeks' ideas about binary gender.

'Minotaur', in the original Greek myths, is a term for the specific individual (also given the name Asterion, or 'starlike', presumably as his proper name), but has since become a generic term for any half-bull, half-human creature in fiction.

While this is the first appearance of a Minotaur proper in **Doctor Who**, Minotaurs or Minotaur-like creatures would turn up in many future **Doctor Who** stories, notably *The Time Monster* (1972), *The Horns of Nimon* (1979-80), and *The God Complex* (2011).

While some of this may be due to the fact that a Minotaur costume is a relatively cheap one, consisting as it does only of a bull's head worn by an otherwise-normal man (and it's certainly no coincidence that *The Time Monster* and *The Horns of Nimon* are both notoriously cheap-looking stories), I suspect it also has to do with what they represent.

The Minotaur is a half-man, half-beast creature, and so like many **Doctor Who** monsters it represents a distorted or 'unnatural' version of humanity – however, most of the popular recurring monsters tend to be those in which humanity has been lessened by becoming more machine-like (the Daleks or Cybermen being the most obvious examples, but even the 'cold-blooded' Silurians and Ice Warriors or regimented, cloned Sontarans would fit to a lesser extent). The Minotaur represents something slightly different, which the programme has otherwise largely lacked – a monster in which humanity is reduced by becoming more emotional and bestial.

And the Minotaur in its classical form is also defeated in a way that is totally different to the defeats of those other monsters. While the Daleks or Cybermen are often defeated by the use of emotion, the Minotaur is defeated by the use of logic and puzzle-solving in the face of emotion – for example, in *The God Complex*, the Minotaur is defeated by destroying Amy's unthinking faith. (It's notable that the series' next attempt to do a Minotaur story after *The Mind Robber*, *The Krotons*, in which the Minotaur is replaced by machine-creatures, does not use this trope – it only works when a bestial creature is being fought.)

In this respect, the Minotaur being defeated by the Doctor and Zoe realising that he is mythical fits perfectly with the figure's larger symbolism – a creature of pure emotion that can only be defeated by cold, logical, thinking.

The Medusa (Sue Pulford)

Medusa, like the Minotaur, is a figure from Greek myth, and like him has become a generic name to be applied to a type of monster, rather than to an individual. In the myth, Medusa was one of three sisters, the Gorgons, but while the other two sisters were immortal, Medusa was able to die. All three of the sisters, however, shared two attributes – instead of hair, their heads had living snakes growing out of them, and if anyone looked at them, that person would immediately turn to stone.

Medusa was killed by the hero Perseus, in a story which seems horrific to modern sensibilities – Medusa was cursed with her appearance for the 'crime' of being raped by a god, Poseidon, in a temple dedicated to another god, Athene. Perseus was then helped by the gods, including Athene, to decapitate Medusa, while she was pregnant with Poseidon's child[64].

Medusa is here presented as a rather straightforward monster, rather than an actual character, yet it's interesting to notice that her nature, in being able to turn people from one mode of existence (flesh) to another (stone), is much like the major threat of the story as a whole, being turned from reality into fiction.

It is possible that the use of a Gorgon in the story may have been inspired by a then-recent film, Hammer's *The Gorgon* (1964). While *The Gorgon* was unlikely to be familiar to the young audience for **Doctor Who**, it featured Patrick Troughton in a major role, which may have brought it to mind.

Medusa is also unique in 1960s **Doctor Who** in being created entirely using stop-motion animation, an effect which had never previously been used in the series.

Cyrano de Bergerac (David Cannon)

Cyrano de Bergerac is the first real person we come across here. Or at least, he is a character with a basis in reality.

Savinien de Cyrano de Bergerac was a 17th-century novelist and soldier, but the character we see here is, rather than the real

---

[64] Poseidon was also responsible for Pasiphaë developing an overwhelming lust for a bull, and thus conceiving the Minotaur. One gets the impression that Poseidon was viciously misogynist, even by the standards of the ancient Greeks, and that a lot of trouble could have been avoided if the other gods had done something about his barbaric attitude towards women.

Savinien, the creation of 19th-century French playwright Edmond Rostand.

Rostand's play *Cyrano de Bergerac* (1897) was very loosely based on the life of the real man, about whom relatively little is known, but was fictionalised to the point that the most memorable aspects of the play bear no relation to anything in the real Cyrano's life.

In Rostand's play, Cyrano has a massive, grotesque nose, and is convinced that this renders him so ugly that he can never be loved by a woman, although he is in love with his cousin, Roxane. When he discovers that Christian de Neuvillette, a fellow cadet serving in the army with him, is in love with Roxane, but is unable to express himself clearly, he writes love letters for Christian to sign and tells Christian what to say in order to woo her.

Roxane falls in love with Christian, but later tells him that she has grown to love him for his soul and would love him even were he ugly. Christian dies in the war, and Cyrano doesn't reveal the truth about the letters' authorship to Roxanne, in order to preserve his memory. However, when Cyrano is dying, Roxane realises that he was the author (although he denies it to the last), and that she loved him all along – and has thus lost him twice, once when Christian died, and now again.

While the real Cyrano did have a large nose (though not the exceptionally deformed proboscis that is seen in most productions of Rostand's play[65]), and he did have a cousin who married de

---

[65] It is possible that Rostand chose to focus his play on Cyrano's nose as a comment on the famous Dreyfus affair which was shaking Parisian society at the time the play premiered. Alfred Dreyfus –

Neuvillette, he was, as far as can be ascertained, as far as possible from the chaste, lovelorn, figure of the play. According to Nicholas Cronk[66]:

> 'he was, in both senses of the word – sexual and intellectual – a libertine. His reputation for debauchery was early established (he wrote a painfully graphic poem about his syphilis) and the tempestuous breakup of his homosexual affair with Dassoucy was much publicized. No less scandalous, however, and not entirely unconnected, was his attachment to the clandestine circle of atheistic free-thinkers then active in Paris...'

The real Cyrano was thus more the romantic poet than romantic hero, and it seems appropriate that the fictional Cyrano should use de Neuvillette almost as a puppet, reciting lines that aren't his, since this is what Rostand is in turn doing to Cyrano.

---

like the Cyrano of the play, a military officer – had been falsely accused of sending letters to the German embassy containing military secrets. Dreyfus was, in fact, framed by a military court to cover up the real culprit. Dreyfus was Jewish, and his case became the nucleus of a larger argument between reactionary, anti-Semitic, militarist monarchists on one side and liberals, socialists, Protestants, and republicans on the other, about how France should define itself as a nation. Rostand was a supporter of Dreyfus, and to present a patriotic soldier with the stereotypically Jewish feature of a large nose, in a play centring on letters attributed to someone other than their real author, was not a very subtle message in late-1890s Paris.

[66] In the introduction to Rostand, Edmond, *Cyrano de Bergerac* (1996).

But even the real, as opposed to the fictional, Cyrano, blurred the lines between his real and fictitious identities. Much of Cyrano's work is lost, but among the surviving works we have is his posthumously published *Histoire comique par Monsieur de Cyrano Bergerac, contenant les états et empires de la lune* ('M Cyrano de Bergerac's Comical History, Containing the States and Empires of the Moon') (1657) and its unfinished sequel, *Fragment d'histoire comique par Monsieur de Cyrano Bergerac, contenant les états et empires du soleil* ('Fragment of M Cyrano de Bergerac's Comical History, Containing the States and Empires of the Sun') (1662).

Both of these are satirical stories of fantastical voyages to other worlds, featuring Cyrano himself as the hero. In these works, Cyrano travels to other planets by means of his own inventions (including, in the former, the first known description of a space journey by rocket), and meets the inhabitants, including at least one character, Domingo Gonsales, from another, earlier, fictional work[67].

While these are regarded by many (notably Roberts) as being prototypical science fiction novels, they are also philosophical works, written as a means of discussing the heresies of Giordano Bruno, who had been executed 19 years before Cyrano's birth for putting forward a view of the universe as being infinite in extent and containing multiple worlds, all as important as the Earth. Cyrano's works take Bruno's speculations as their starting point, and contain much frank advocacy of atheism and speculation on

---

[67] Godwin, Francis, *The Man in the Moone or the Discourse of a Voyage thither by Domingo Gonsales* (1638).

the formation of the solar system and the nature of the universe, some of it remarkably correct (the claim that were we to stand on Jupiter or Saturn we would be able to see other 'worlds' not visible from Earth), other parts rather less so (the contention that the reason America was not discovered earlier was that it had only recently been spat out of the sun as detritus).

These works inspired Swift when writing *Gulliver's Travels*, but the parallels with *The Mind Robber* itself are intriguing – a space traveller and inventor who travels to another world and there meets characters from fiction – as is the way the character of Cyrano, in Rostand's play, acts as a ghostwriter for de Neuvillette.

Blackbeard (Gerry Wain)

Blackbeard is another character who is based strongly on a real person. The real 'Blackbeard', Edward Teach (probably not his real name), was a pirate who for about a year commanded a small fleet of stolen ships, before being killed in a battle with Virginian colony authorities.

Much of what we know about Teach comes from *A General History of the Robberies and Murders of the Most Notorious Pyrates* (1724), a pseudonymous book written by 'Charles Johnson', which is often attributed to Daniel Defoe. This book came out at the high point of success for stories of maritime adventure – Defoe's *Robinson Crusoe* (1719) was first published five years earlier, while *Gulliver's Travels* came out only two years later – and is the main source for Teach having used the name 'Blackbeard'.

It's possible that the character of Blackbeard was brought to mind by the release of the massively successful Disney film *Blackbeard's Ghost* in early 1968 – the film was one of the biggest hits of the year, and it is likely that the children watching **Doctor Who** would have been aware of it.

Blackbeard, like Cyrano, Lancelot, and d'Argtanan, is only introduced briefly, at the climax of the story, in a single fight scene. As the story moves towards its end, more and more of the characters introduced are based on real people, rather than on purely fictional characters. Intentional or not, this increases the sense of threat as the story builds towards its climax, and reminds us that it is, within the rules of the Land of Fiction, entirely possible for real people to become fictional characters.

The real Edward Teach had a far less auspicious career than any of the other real people fictionalised in *The Mind Robber*, being a rather unsuccessful pirate captain, with a short career ending in his death. But Teach **appeared** fearsome – 'such a figure that imagination cannot form an idea of a fury from hell to look more frightful'[68] – and so even after his brief career was at an end, he was spoken of as particularly vicious and horrifying, despite there being no known evidence of him ever having killed. The Blackbeard of legend was thus the creation of the rather less imposing real man.

Lancelot (John Greenwood)

Lancelot is the sole representative in this story of the Arthurian legends which make up such a large part of the British imaginative landscape. Like many of the characters we have seen so far, Lancelot is French in origin, appearing first in the 12th-century

---

[68] Johnson, Charles, *A General History of the Robberies and Murders of the Most Notorious Pyrates* (1724), p54.

works of Chrétien de Troyes, though various attempts have been made to suggest earlier origins for the character in Irish or Welsh legend (none particularly convincingly).

Lancelot would have been familiar to the older viewers of the story from the successful TV series **The Adventures of Sir Lancelot** (1956-57), which had been popular in the late 1950s, and had starred William Russell, who had gone on to appear as the Doctor's companion Ian Chesterton in **Doctor Who** from its first episode, 'An Unearthly Child' (*An Unearthly Child* episode 1, 1963) until 'The Planet of Decision' (*The Chase* episode 6, 1965).

More recently, though, the character had appeared in the musical *Camelot* (1967), a film version of which had been released in 1967 to great success, and which had focussed on the character, his relationship with King Arthur and his adultery with Arthur's wife Guinevere. Once again we see a character from a story that is many centuries old, but which had recently come back into the public consciousness thanks to a film version.

The Karkus (Christopher Robbie)

The Karkus is a superhero who appears in the *Hourly Telepress*...

The character is actually the only one who is an in-universe fiction – rather than being a character (like the Doctor or Zoe) who is meant to be 'real' within the story (though we will look later at the extent to which those characters actually **are** meant to be 'real'...) or a character from fiction we know about, he's a character who appears in fiction within the fictional world of the story. This makes him the only fictional character in the story who the Doctor is unaware of. All the classic fiction to which we have access, the

Doctor has read – but he's not read the adventures of the Karkus, which we have also not read.

The Karkus is, of course, intended as a parody of the Adam West-starring **Batman** (1966-68) TV show[69], which had been a massive hit in the previous couple of years (though its popularity was on the wane slightly – as, indeed, was **Doctor Who**'s during this period), and which had been scheduled against **Doctor Who** by many ITV regions, in an attempt to win some of its audience away[70].

The parody is somewhat blunted by the strange decision to have the Karkus played with a strong Mitteleuropean accent (which now makes one think rather of Rainier Wolfcastle, the parody of Arnold Schwarzenegger in **The Simpsons** (1989-)), but parodying **Batman** was an odd choice in itself. The programme was a self-parody from the start, playing everything with a wink to the camera, with Adam West's absolutely straight heroic turn, performed in much the same manner as William Shatner's Captain Kirk, being one of the most knowing, camp performances on TV.

---

[69] According to *The Complete History* #13, the costume designs state he has a 'Batman-type outfit' (p19). The information text on the DVD release of *The Mind Robber* also states that **Batman** was the inspiration, at the Karkus' first appearance. The animated stars when the Karkus appears, in particular, are in the style of the American series.

[70] And they did appeal to much of the same audience, at least anecdotally – the present author's father once said, when talking about the lack of entertainment during his 1960s childhood, 'the only things that were on that you'd ever want to watch were **The Monkees** [1966-68], **Doctor Who**, and **Batman**'.

In fact it's interesting to contrast West's style of performance with Troughton's. West's Batman is put in implausible situations with stock adventure plots, takes the situation absolutely seriously, and as a result the programme is (for those who like it, which I largely do) extremely funny. Troughton, meanwhile, is put in similar situations and turns in a largely comic performance (less so than the folk-memory of his Doctor as 'a clown', but still the closest anyone has come, other than Tom Baker in his later years, to playing the Doctor as a comedy character). Yet his performance is one of the things that makes the show so effective when it ventures, as it so often did in his tenure, into horror.

Of course, Troughton's performance is far more nuanced than West's — West's is deliberately one-note, while Troughton is, at least in his better stories, allowed to express his full, wide, range — but the contrast between the techniques does point to the basic difference between the two programmes, and to the problem with **Doctor Who** parodying **Batman**.

Batman could, had audiences in the USA been sufficiently aware of **Doctor Who** at the time, have parodied it easily within its own format — just have a Doctor-substitute character turn up and behave exactly as the Doctor always does, and within the format and fictional world of **Batman** the character would be inherently ridiculous. On the other hand, **Doctor Who**, at least at this point in time, needs to scare children, and so its parody of Batman has to be at least superficially threatening, rather than purely ludicrous.

The Karkus, then, is a misconceived parody, but something of the type is utterly necessary for the plot of *The Mind Robber*. The Doctor needs to be shown to be fallible, for there to be any element of danger at all, and there needs to be at least one threat that can't just be dealt with by saying 'it's not real'. That threat also needs to be one that is unfamiliar to the audience, because otherwise the Doctor is seen to know less than them, which would undercut the whole conception of the character. Thus, the Karkus – a character that is clearly a known type, so recognisable as fictional, but who is not specifically known to the viewer.

D'Artagnan (John Greenwood)

Charles de Batz-Castelmore d'Artagnan is another fictionalised real person – a contemporary of Cyrano de Bergerac, and like him a French aristocrat, but one with very different attitudes. While Cyrano was an atheist rebel, d'Artagnan was captain of the King's Musketeers, and later Governor of Lille, as establishment a figure as it is possible to imagine.

D'Artagnan is, of course, also the hero of the doubly-fictionalised *The Three Musketeers* (1844), by Alexandre Dumas père and Auguste Maquet[71]. Dumas' novel itself blurs the lines between fiction and reality. In the author's preface, the book is claimed to be a newly-discovered manuscript, *Memoirs of the Comte de la Fere, Touching Some Events Which Passed in France Toward the End of the Reign of King Louis XIII and the Commencement of the Reign of King Louis XIV*. The 'discovery' of this book, in turn, had

---

[71] Dumas is the only credited author, but by most accounts of the partnership Maquet laid down much of the groundwork for the novel. While this was not widely known at the time *The Mind Robber* was made, it is interesting that this book raises many of the same questions of its own authorship that the other works discussed here do.

been inspired by Dumas reading *Les Mémoires de M d'Artagnan* by Gatien de Courtilz de Sandras (1700), an historical novel based around the life of d'Artagnan, which in the preface Dumas affects to believe to be the real memoirs of the historical figure.

Thus *The Three Musketeers* is a fiction pretending to be a non-fictional memoir, based on a fiction pretending to be a non-fictional memoir, based on the life of a real person, 'written' by a great author whose most famous works are actually written by an almost-unknown ghost writer. A more appropriate story to be referenced in a story about turning real people into fictions, and about a hidden mind controlling things from behind the scenes, is hard to imagine.

The Three Musketeers would have been familiar to viewers thanks to a 1966 TV adaptation by the BBC, starring Brian Blessed, Jeremy Brett, and Jeremy Young.

The White Robots

The white robots used in the story were originally created for a now-lost episode of the science fiction anthology series **Out of the Unknown**, broadcast in 1967, and were reused primarily because they didn't require any new expenditure (other than a coat of paint).

It's therefore questionable whether they are intended as fictional characters in the narrative itself. David Maloney, for example, didn't realise when filming the serial that they had not been purpose-built for it[72].

---

[72] *The Complete History* #13, p26.

However, it's certainly possible that viewers in 1968 would have recognised the robots from their original appearance, in the episode *The Prophet* (1967).

This episode was based on the Isaac Asimov story 'Reason' (1941), and it's interesting to note given the themes we have been discussing that it involves a rebellious artificial intelligence that has, through a supposedly-logical process, come to believe in a deity that created robots – yet another example of pure logic going astray. Even more coincidentally, the robot's deity was called 'the Master'.

The **Out of the Unknown** episode is unlikely to have been a direct influence on *The Mind Robber* other than in providing the robots, but it's interesting to note that these themes were very much considered within the normal bounds of what televised science fiction did in the mid-1960s.

The Toy Soldiers

While no source for these has been noted, a performance of the Tchaikovsky ballet *The Nutcracker* (1892), which features toy soldiers coming to life, was shown on BBC Two on 10 March 1968[73]. Ling's original draft had 'brain creatures', which were revised into the toy soldiers at some point between 26 February and 26 March[74], so it's reasonable to assume that they were inspired by this performance.

---

[73] 'BBC Genome Project'.
[74] *The Complete History* #13, p18.

The Master (Emrys Jones)

The Master is a writer of children's fiction, based in part on Ling's experiences writing for *The Eagle* (1950-69)[75], to which he contributed the (text-only) school serial 'The Three J's', about the fictional Northbrook School, for six years.

Ling also, however, based the character on Charles Hamilton, who under the pseudonym 'Frank Richards' and others such as 'Martin Clifford', 'Owen Conquest', and 'Ralph Redway' may be the most prolific author who ever lived. Hamilton wrote school stories, of the same type as Ling's serial, for boys' papers such as *The Gem* (1907-39) and *The Magnet* (1908-40), in an extremely pared-down, repetitive style, described by George Orwell as:

> 'easily imitated – an extraordinary, artificial, repetitive style, quite different from anything else now existing in English literature [...] The first thing that anyone would notice is the extraordinary amount of tautology [...] seemingly designed to spin out the story, but actually playing its part in creating the atmosphere. For the same reason various facetious expressions are repeated over and over again [...] The slang ('Go and eat coke!', 'What the thump!', 'You frabjous ass!',

---

[75] A children's comic, featuring uplifting, wholesome, boys'-own adventures, designed to instil Christian morality into young boys, which nonetheless managed to become the most popular British adventure comic by quite some way, largely thanks to the strip 'Dan Dare: Pilot of the Future'. The **Dan Dare** strip has been widely credited for inspiring much of Terry Nation's **Doctor Who** work, and Dr Who, as played by Peter Cushing, can be seen reading an issue of *The Eagle* in the film *Dr Who and the Daleks* (1965).

etc etc) has never been altered, so that the boys are now using slang which is at least 30 years out of date. In addition, the various nicknames are rubbed in on every possible occasion [...] There is a constant, untiring effort to keep the atmosphere intact and to make sure that every new reader learns immediately who is who.'[76]

Orwell believed that this style was because the works had to be produced by a team of writers, saying in his essay:

'The stories in the *Magnet* are signed "Frank Richards" and those in the *Gem*, "Martin Clifford", but a series lasting 30 years could hardly be the work of the same person every week.'[77]

In fact, they were all the work of the same man (although occasional other writers stepped in to write fill-in stories under the same pseudonyms), who wrote over 100 million words of fiction in a career that lasted from 1896 to 1961, and is widely credited as the most prolific author of all time.

While the Master claims his output was 'probably some kind of a record', it's nothing near Hamilton's. His 5,000 words a week is slightly above the average for professional writers, and while Zoe's 'that's well over half a million words!'[78] is an order of magnitude

---

[76] Orwell, *Essays*, p188. **Doctor Who** fans may note that Terrance Dicks used a very similar technique to aid in his own prodigious output of novelisations for Target, although Dicks had the advantage of working from already-written scripts.
[77] Orwell, *Essays*, p188.
[78] Episode 4.

out (if he wrote 5,000 words per week for 25 years, that would be approximately six and a half million words), his output would be impressive, but hardly record-breaking. But the implication is clearly that he is intended to be hugely prolific, and he is intended to recall Hamilton's more staggering output.

He is also intended to resemble Hamilton physically. In his later years, Hamilton was white-haired and wore a skullcap in all photos, covering up his extensive bald patch. The description of the Master in the costume design notes states 'He is a dear little old gentleman: benign and white-haired, wearing spectacles and a skullcap...'[79]

However, the stories described by the Master don't match either Hamilton's work or Ling's own. The magazine for which he claims to have written, *The Ensign*, did not exist (despite claims otherwise by some fan sources), but the stories he describes are far more similar to the adventure serials by non-Hamilton authors used as filler material in *Gem* and *Magnet* than the school stories for which Hamilton was known.

The character he describes writing, 'Captain Jack Harkaway'[80], does however share a name with a character, Jack Harkaway, who was

---

[79] *The Complete History* #13, p19.

[80] This name naturally leads to a certain amount of speculation among the more Watsonian contingent of **Doctor Who** fandom that the Master was inspired in his creation by the similarly-named time-travelling adventurer Captain Jack Harkness, who appeared as a regular character in **Doctor Who** from 2005 to 2010. While this is fun to speculate about, however, it is clearly not anything to do with the story as written and produced in 1968.

the popular hero of several late-19th-century penny dreadfuls, starting with *Jack Harkaway's School Days*, serialised in the publication *Boys of England* (1867-1900), which was later retitled *Boys of England and Jack Harkaway's Journal of Travel, Fun and Instruction*. The character even had a single-reel silent film, *The Childhood of Jack Harkaway* (1910) made about him[81].

However, while Hamilton and the penny dreadful writers were the most obvious source of inspiration for the character of the Master, Ling was also inspired by a more prosaic source – the viewers of **Crossroads** would often write letters to the show asking for work, not as actors or production staff, but as waitresses in the fictional motel in the soap opera[82]. At the time it was common for viewers of soaps, in a time when television was a relatively new medium, and when much less behind-the-scenes information was available, to believe, often quite fervently, that what they were watching was in some way real. Stories abound of actors in villainous roles being accosted in the street by viewers, or actors in more sympathetic roles being warned about unsuitable relationships into which their characters were entering.

And this confusion of fictional character and real life seems, as we have seen, to be replicated in the choices of characters represented. With the exception of Sir Lancelot, all the non-monster characters in one way or another represent some blurring of the lines between author, fictional creation, and real life, so it's

---

[81] I have, however, been able to find no evidence that this Jack Harkaway ever attained the rank of captain, despite some claims in fan sources.
[82] Howe, Stammers and Walker, *The Handbook*, p261.

appropriate that the final conflict of the story should be with a character who is a fictionalised version of a real author (an author who similarly fictionalised himself, by the use of pen-names and, in the later years of his life, once he gained belated fame, a careful control of his public image), but who also represents the author of the script. The Master is both Ling and Hamilton – and Hamilton's creation 'Frank Richards' – but he is also a character in his own right, whose biographical details match neither man.

In a story where the threat is for the real to become fictional, the primary antagonist is a real man who has become fictionalised multiple times over, both in-story and in reality. Orwell believed, until corrected, that Hamilton didn't even exist at all and was a team of authors writing in similar style. What better fate for a man who hid behind multiple identities so well that each of those identities was in turn believed to hide multiple individuals, than to disappear from reality altogether and become a pure fiction?

DANGEROUS TOYS

One thing that many writers have noted about *The Mind Robber* is its similarity to the story *The Celestial Toymaker,* a story from season three, which had featured William Hartnell's Doctor.

The Celestial Toymaker is a story whose reputation has lost a lot of its lustre in recent years, largely because the soundtrack being available has allowed people to hear that it is not, as fan memory had it, a fascinating and complex fantasy, but rather a tedious bore. While Cornell, Topping, and Day, writing before the soundtrack was widely available, say: 'Doctor Who's first stab at surrealism is an unqualified success, taking the symbols of childhood and turning them into a nightmarish prototype of **The Crystal Maze**'[83], many later writers[84] argue that at best the story has a kernel of a good idea, ineptly presented, and at worst that it is one of the dullest pieces of television ever created.

They're not wrong. Much like *The Mind Robber, The Celestial Toymaker* is a story whose production was beset with problems. The difference is that while the problems in *The Mind Robber* caused the production team to rise to the occasion, those afflicting

---

[83] Cornell, Day and Topping, *The Discontinuity Guide*, p56.
[84] Notably Perryman, Neil, and Sue Perryman, *The Wife In Space volume #1:The Miserable Git* (2015), (p193); Sandifer, Philip, *TARDIS Eruditorum #1: William Hartnell* (2011), pp320-330; Shearman, Robert, and Toby Hadoke, *Running Through Corridors: Rob and Toby's Marathon Watch of Doctor Who – Volume 1: The 60s* (2010), pp146-151; and Wood, Tat, and Lawrence Miles, *About Time: The Unauthorized Guide to Doctor Who #1 – 1963-1966: Seasons 1 to 3* (2006), p256.

The Celestial Toymaker seem at every point to have made the production team say 'Oh well, this'll have to do', and go for the easiest possible option.

Thus while *The Celestial Toymaker*'s basic idea – the Doctor, Steven, and Dodo are transported to a nightmarish realm, presided over by a godlike figure who makes them play deadly games with their survival at stake – is an excellent one on paper, the show as broadcast (at least as far as we can tell from the one surviving episode and the audio recordings of the rest) is quite extraordinarily dull, consisting mostly of the Doctor playing 'the Trilogic game' (a simple puzzle better known as the Tower of Hanoi), and the Toymaker occasionally actually helping the Doctor win, just in case the story were to accidentally develop any kind of suspense.

But the underlying threat of *The Celestial Toymaker* is very similar to that in *The Mind Robber* – the various characters with which the Toymaker populates his games are people who have failed his earlier tests, and have been turned into versions of stereotypical characters from fiction. Most notably, the schoolboy 'Cyril' is so clearly based on Billy Bunter that the BBC had to issue a disclaimer denying the characters were the same, in order to avoid the possibility of lawsuits from the Charles Hamilton estate.

Another link comes with the disappearance of the Doctor. The Doctor spends much of the story invisible, only returning to visibility near the end, and the plan was that when the Doctor reappeared, he would have a new face, and this would be how William Hartnell was written out of the series and replaced[85].

Whether this is true or not, the idea of recasting (temporarily, in this case) after a character is manipulated by a powerful force was one that **was** used in *The Mind Robber*, when Jamie's face is wrongly recreated by the Doctor, in order to get around Hines' chickenpox.

The Celestial Toymaker is, in other words, very much like a bad first draft of *The Mind Robber*, or its mirror image – a version of a very similar story in which everything went wrong instead of right. It's a cautionary tale that shows that high concepts are not enough. *The Mind Robber* is not a great **Doctor Who** story because it has the idea of the Land of Fiction in it, but because it follows up on that idea and does interesting things with it, and does so with a sense of storytelling, and an aesthetic sensibility, entirely alien to the earlier story.

In this book, we have largely concentrated on the ideas behind *The Mind Robber*, but it is important to note that ideas need to be realised. We are not looking, here, at a Platonic ideal of a **Doctor Who** serial, but one made in the real world, by real people – writers, a director, actors, set designers, camera operators – all of whom had to make myriad decisions, small and large, which make up the final programme as it exists today. Had they made different choices, a story that has become one of the most admired pieces of

---

[85] 'With regard to *The Toymaker* we wanted to experiment with the ways to change from Bill to another actor...' (Donald Tosh, interviewed in Stevens, Alan, 'Donald Tosh Interview').

telefantasy of the 1960s could easily have been, instead, a ridiculous piece of dull camp.

THE MALE GAZE, OR THAT SCENE

While I would not want to spend too much time on the subject, it is impossible to discuss *The Mind Robber* without someone bringing up the subject of 'Zoe's arse', as it is almost invariably put.

The scene in question comes at the end of episode 1, when the TARDIS has been disintegrated, and the console is spinning through a vacuum with the two companions prone upon it. Zoe is wearing a particularly tight costume, and is posed in such a way that for much of the scene the camera is focused on her posterior. Both Hines and Padbury note[86] that the scene has been mentioned to them on many occasions by fans, all noting this fact.

This could be viewed as a mere accident of shot composition – there are, after all, only so many ways one can pose two people clinging to a TARDIS console in an otherwise-blank void, and given the tight schedule to which the programme was made, it could well be that nobody considered how this scene would look. Certainly nobody making the programme could possibly have guessed that it would be watched and analysed over and again almost 50 years after production.

But at the same time, the role of the female companion in **Doctor Who** has often been a sexualised one, and this trend seems to start around the time Zoe first appears in the series (although it doesn't help in this regard that zip fasteners seem to have a habit of malfunctioning around Wendy Padbury, so some shots that appear sexualised genuinely aren't intended that way).

---

[86] In the special features for the DVD release of *The Mind Robber*.

A phrase has been attributed to several different **Doctor Who** producers[87] – 'something for the dads'. For much of its existence, **Doctor Who** has been aimed at a family audience, and so different elements of the show have been designed to appeal to different members of the audience. And that audience was believed to include adult men, who had been watching **Grandstand** (1958-2007), a sports programme which was on directly before **Doctor Who** for much of its 20th-century existence. Those men were believed to be watching primarily for their children's sake, but it was nonetheless important that, as members of the viewing audience, there be something in the series for them to enjoy as well.

Thus, 'something for the dads' – the companion as sexualised young woman, often scantily dressed, for the men in the audience to... appreciate, may be the politest way to put it.

While overt sexual content is almost nonexistent in 20th century **Doctor Who**, and so this sexualisation is often regarded as 'innocent fun', the fact is that at several points in the series, the composition of shots and sometimes the plot itself are distorted to provide an excuse for focussing on companions' bodies as sexual objects. Particularly egregious examples include the reduction of Leela to her underwear in *The Talons of Weng-Chiang* (1977), Nyssa

---

[87] I have seen this attributed to producers Innes Lloyd and John Nathan-Turner, and script editor Terrance Dicks, but never authoritatively or in the form of an actual quote. One suspects that the phrase, which has become a common part of fan-lore, accurately reflects the attitude of several production staff, but was not actually spoken within the production office.

similarly stripping down in *Terminus* (1983), and the focus on Peri's breasts during the regeneration scene in episode 4 of *The Caves of Androzani* (1984). That in two of these three cases the directors were among the most accomplished ever to work on the series (Maloney on *Talons* and Graeme Harper on *Androzani*), working on two of the most acclaimed serials in the history of the show, shows that this was a deliberate choice made by skilled people who knew what they were doing, not merely accident or thoughtlessness.

In this light, the sexualisation of the companion is troubling. Terrance Dicks, who was assistant script editor on *The Mind Robber* and edited or wrote a vast number of **Doctor Who** scripts and books over the decades following it, has often stated that the purpose of the female companion in **Doctor Who** is to get tied to the railway tracks. The companion has very little agency for much of the series, and the sexualisation of the companions too often feeds into that. While it is far from the case that all sexualised imagery of women is objectifying, in the case of **Doctor Who** it very often is – the female characters are all too often treated as objects, rather than as people.

And so it's a shame that in a story which is entirely *about* agency, and identity, and free will, and about the danger of turning people into objects, and in which the female companion has rather more characterisation than many of her successors, a story that's filled with astonishing juxtapositions and fascinating ideas, the most memorable image for many viewers is of the outline of Wendy Padbury's buttocks in a tight spangly catsuit.

IS THE DOCTOR A RENEGADE FROM THE LAND OF FICTION?

No.

OK... a more thorough answer is perhaps needed. Some recent analyses of *The Mind Robber*, notably Philip Sandifer's[88], have pointed to Gulliver's line to the Doctor in episode 2, 'He has articles of impeachment against you for treason and other capital crimes,' as evidence that the Doctor is, at least in this story, intended to be a refugee from the Land of Fiction, escaped into the real world, and thus committing treason against it.

This seems a very attractive notion on the surface – after all, the Doctor **is** a fictional creation, and for those of us who prefer to see the Doctor as a more mercurial figure, and who don't like too much of his background to be tied down to specific places and events, it's an elegant way to give him a permanent air of mystery. Whatever else is revealed about him becomes merely the context that the fictional character stepped into when he became real.

Unfortunately, there's nothing in the story to support this interpretation. The relevant section of dialogue is:

GULLIVER

I said, beware false traitor, highwayman, robber, pickpocket, murderer.

---

[88] Sandifer, Philip, *Patrick Troughton* (2012), pp215-222.

DOCTOR

I think you must be making some mistake. Highwayman, indeed?

[...]

GULLIVER

Well sir, if you can assure me you are no traitor.

DOCTOR

Now how can I be a traitor when I don't even know where I am? Where am I?

[...]

GULLIVER

He has articles of impeachment against you for treason and other capital crimes.

DOCTOR

Treason again. Really.

GULLIVER

I leave you to your prudence what measures you will take.

It's clear from the exchange that the Doctor finds the accusation of treason ridiculous, and more importantly that he has no idea where he is – he doesn't recognise the Land of Fiction when he arrives there, and seems to have relatively little understanding of it even once he becomes aware of its nature. This is in itself not conclusive, but it is certainly suggestive. The intention of the scene as written and shot is clearly that Gulliver's accusations make little sense to the Doctor.

It is, in short, not meant to be hinting at the origins of **the Doctor**, but rather of **Gulliver**, who at this time we only know as 'the Stranger'. Gulliver's strange phrasing, which makes no sense in its specifics, but only as a general warning that the Doctor is thought of by the Master as a danger, is meant to be a clue. We know that the Doctor is not a traitor (or indeed a pickpocket, highwayman, or murderer – he has on occasion been seen to steal things, so the accusation of robbery might be seen as a fair one), so the accusations are false – but those who know *Gulliver's Travels* may well remember the phrases which Gulliver is speaking.

But could the accusation of treachery nonetheless be true? True, the Doctor doesn't recognise the Land at that moment, but he could just not yet realise he's back 'home'.

The problem with this is that the accusation is not made anywhere else in the entire story. It's a fun idea to play with – the Doctor as a refugee from the Land of Fiction, running off to become a real boy like Pinocchio – but there is simply no support for it in the work as written or transmitted, and nor is there any extra-textual evidence that this was the intent of anyone involved in the story's production. It's not completely inconsistent with anything we see on screen, but it requires a large stretch to reconcile it with the programme we're actually watching.

While I am far from against wildly speculative ideas about **Doctor Who**, as the rest of this book testifies, the idea that the Doctor is some sort of living story, an embodiment of fiction itself, escaped into the real world, owes more to a combination of mystical thinking and the almost idolatrous way in which **Doctor Who** is viewed by some fans.

There is a common claim in fandom that any story worth telling can be told as a **Doctor Who** story, to which the obvious retort is that *Ulysses* (1922) would not be improved by the addition of some Daleks, and Proust's search for lost time would be rather shorter if a man in a blue box turned up and took him back to the time the madeleine evoked. The idea of the Doctor himself being from the Land owes more to this claim than to any serious analysis of the story.

The Doctor in this story may not yet be a Time Lord from Gallifrey, but nor is he a character from the Land of Fiction. Fundamentally, the story shows the idealised characters of the Land to be flawed because they lack depth (sometimes literally, as when characters are turned into cardboard cutouts, but always metaphorically), and shows the real world, in all its messiness, as being superior to the smoothed-out, controlled, orderly world of fiction, with its tin soldiers marching in step and characters who can only say the same words they've already said.

Troughton's Doctor is the messiest and most anarchic of all Doctors. His conception of the character is too physical to be reduced to an ideal. A version of his Doctor that came from the Land of Fiction would be more like the fan idea of 'the second Doctor', constantly spouting catchphrases like 'when I say run, run!' and 'oh my giddy Aunt!', than the Doctor that appears on our screen.

Everything about this story points to the real as superior to the ideal. To read it as saying its hero is an idealised spirit made flesh is to badly misread a character who is more mess than messiah.

APPENDIX: REVISITING THE LAND OF FICTION

While the Land of Fiction has not yet been brought back in the TV series, the wide range of **Doctor Who** tie-in materials, in book and audio drama form, have on occasion returned to it as a setting for further adventures, usually with little artistic success. The Land of Fiction has turned up in two major tie-in series – the Virgin **New Adventures** series of novels, and Big Finish Productions' line of audio dramas featuring the Doctor – as well as in numerous fan works.

New Adventures

The New Adventures was a book series that ran from 1991 to 1997, featuring the Doctor[89] in adventures that were intended as a direct continuation of the television series, picking up shortly after the end of *Survival* (1989) and supposedly following a 'masterplan' laid down for the TV series by script editor Andrew Cartmel before its cancellation. In actual fact, the books quickly diverged from the tone set by the TV series, becoming much 'darker' (in the way that only genre fiction aimed at young men in the 1990s can be dark) and with more complex plots befitting the medium.

The 22nd novel in the range, *Conundrum* by Steve Lyons, was something of an exception. Rather than the dark grittiness of the bulk of the range, Lyons goes for a light comedic tone here (as

---

[89] It continued until 1999, but for the last two years it did not feature the Doctor, concentrating instead on companion Bernice Summerfield, who had been created for the range.

befitting a writer whose main credit to this point was writing for the *Red Dwarf Smegazine* (1992-94)), and creates what was for the time a very metafictional story indeed[90], one where the narratorial voice is that of the new Master of the Land of Fiction himself. At one point, Ace even not only becomes fictional, but sees actual copies of previous *New Adventures*:

> 'From the battered white cover, a face stared out at her.
>
> 'Her face.
>
> 'She gasped, flinched away, and let the book drop unimpeded to the ground. It landed atop a mound of similar volumes, each emblazoned with the same futuristic logo, with a title beneath. Names like 'Dragonfire', 'Love and War', 'Deceit'. The story of her life, reduced to paperback form. And when her hand went to her face again, she felt not blood this time, but words – dripping impossibly, letter by letter, out through her cuts and down to the floor, where the greedy novels soaked her pain into their bloated pages.'[91]

Conundrum manages actually to be a relatively respectable sequel to *The Mind Robber,* although it does of course have its faults (some down to inexperience – this was Lyons' first novel – and some down to having to fit in with an ongoing storyline in the

---

[90] The BBC Books range which started in 1997 would, with writers such as Paul Magrs and Lawrence Miles, end up making this look rather staid, but in the context of the less formally-experimental **New Adventures** series it was quite surprisingly self-referential.

[91] Lyons, Steve, *Conundrum*, p247.

books which required the TARDIS crew to be thoroughly unpleasant to and unreasonable with each other).

Conundrum in turn spawned its own sequel, also by Lyons and again featuring the Land, *Head Games* (1995), but this was rather less successful, being largely devoted to continuity references and moving on a particularly 'dark' ongoing plot, and having little of *Conundrum*'s lightness of touch.

Big Finish

Big Finish is a company which has, since 1999, produced audio plays on CD (and in its early days cassette, and latterly as downloads). These audio plays are usually full-cast dramas based on well-known British media properties (for example **Judge Dredd**, **Blake's 7**, and **Sapphire and Steel**), and a large number of them are based on **Doctor Who** or its characters and monsters.

Their most successful range is an ongoing monthly series of **Doctor Who** audio stories, starring Peter Davison, Sylvester McCoy, and Colin Baker reprising their roles[92] as the Doctor. In recent years, many of these plays have been organised into trilogies, with two standalone stories teasing subplots which pay off in a third part that relies on the first two for its effect.

The trilogy which started in April 2010 (and which was actually a tetralogy, consisting of three stories in the main range plus a tie-in in Big Finish's **Companion Chronicles** range of narrated audiobooks,

---

[92] Paul McGann has occasionally also featured in this monthly series, but he, Tom Baker, David Tennant and John Hurt have for the most part appeared in other ranges, structured as seasons or specials.

narrated by Hines) saw Colin Baker's Doctor meet up again with Jamie, and deal with Cybermen, the *Titanic*, and the Highland Clearances, before realising that all these events had taken place in the Land of Fiction, which was being invaded by the Cybermen.

In these four stories, *City of Spires, Night's Black Agents, The Wreck of the Titan,* and *Legend of the Cybermen* (all 2010), the possibilities of the Land are more or less wasted, sadly, as it is not revealed until well into the third of the four that the adventures are not taking place in the 'real' world – and indeed that Jamie as portrayed in the CDs is not the Jamie from the TV series, but a fictionalised recreation of him in the Land of Fiction, created by Zoe, who has become the new Master of the Land.

As a result, even when it does become clear that the stories are set in the Land, not much use is made of it as a setting, other than as another place for the Cybermen to stomp into and fail to invade in any real way. *Legend of the Cybermen* does involve several moments when the fourth wall is broken, and knowing lines like 'Pseudohistorical to base under siege; you're quite at home', but it's almost shockingly unmemorable – I listened to it when it came out, and coming back to it five years on when writing this book I had almost no memory of it. Writing this a week after listening again, I find the same problem.

And much the same problem also besets *The Crooked Man* (2014), a story in the company's **Fourth Doctor Adventures** range written by John Dorney, and featuring the fourth Doctor and Leela. In this story, little-known fictional characters are entering the real world through a breach between realities in the small seaside town of East Wold. A good story could be written about the experience of being a forgotten or neglected fictional character, but sadly this isn't it.

Minor Appearances

The Land of Fiction (though not the Doctor) also appeared in a one-off comic-strip in *Doctor Who Magazine,* 'Character Assassin', written by Scott Gray with art by Adrian Salmon. In this story, the Master (the Doctor's Time Lord enemy, not the Master from *The Mind Robber*) tries and fails to join a gentlemen's club for Victorian villains. The story does not admit of much analysis, being only seven pages long, but as the circulation of *Doctor Who Magazine* was rather higher than that of either the **New Adventures** or the Big Finish CDs, it is probably the return to the Land that has been most widely read.

The second Doctor briefly returns to the Land in 'Future Imperfect', a story by Marc Platt in *The Doctor Who Yearbook 1992* (1991). In this story it is 'revealed' that Lemuel Gulliver is really the Gallifreyan Chancellor Goth (a character from *The Deadly Assassin* also played by Bernard Horsfall).

Ultimately, even the best of these returns to the Land suffers from the problem that we're merely revisiting old ground, and not going anywhere new. *Conundrum* succeeds to an extent, because the novel medium is arguably more suited to a story about writing and words than the television is[93], but what we have in general here is

---

[93] Though the extent to which British television in the 1960s was primarily an audio, at least as much as a visual, medium should not be underestimated. One of the reasons we are able to experience the lost **Doctor Who** stories is because fans made audio recordings

old favourite characters turning up to do the same things they've always done, in the same ways, for the same audiences. Had the Doctor been trapped in the Land of Fiction forever, reduced to the same kind of fiction as Gulliver or Rapunzel, these are the kind of stories that would have been told about him.

of the series, and found that the dialogue and sound effects conveyed enough of the story to make them worth preserving and listening to.

BIBLIOGRAPHY

Books

Bechdel, Alison, *Dykes to Watch out For*. Ithaca NY, Firebrand Books, 1986. ISBN 9780932379177.

Bucher-Jones, Simon, *Image of the Fendahl*. **The Black Archive** #5. Edinburgh, Obverse Books, 2016. ISBN 9781909031418.

Carroll, Lewis, *Alice's Adventures in Wonderland*. London, Macmillan, 1865.

Clapham, Mark, Eddie Robson and Jim Smith, *Who's Next: An Unofficial and Unauthorised Guide to Doctor Who*. London, Virgin Publishing, 2005. ISBN 9780753509487.

Cornell, Paul, Martin Day and Keith Topping, *Doctor Who: The Discontinuity Guide*. London, Virgin Publishing, 1995. ISBN 9780426204428.

De Bergerac, Savinien de Cyrano, *Histoire Comique par Monsieur de Cyrano Bergerac, Contenant les Etats et Empires de la Lune*. Paris, Charles de Sercy, 1657.

De Bergerac, Savinien de Cyrano, *Fragment d'histoire comique par Monsieur de Cyrano Bergerac, Contenant les Etats et Empires du Soleil* Paris, Charles de Sercy, 1662.

Dexter, Ray, *Patrick Troughton*. **Doctor Who Episode By Episode** #2. Kindle edition, 2011. ASIN B007HAC6LW.

Dumas, Alexandre, *The Three Musketeers* (*Les Trois Mousquetaires*). Serialised 1844.

Freeman, John, ed, *The Doctor Who Yearbook 1992*. London, Marvel Comics Ltd, 1991. ISBN 9781854002839.

Hickey, Andrew, *Fifty Stories for Fifty Years: An Unauthorised Guide to the Highlights of Doctor Who*. Kindle edition, 2013. ASIN B00GUTXOZS.

Howe, David J, Mark Stammers and Stephen James Walker, *The Handbook: The Unofficial and Unauthorised Guide to the Production of Doctor Who*. Tolworth, Telos Publishing, 2005. ISBN 9781903889596.

Johnson, Captain Charles, *A General History of the Robberies and Murders of the Most Notorious Pyrates*. London, Ch Rivington, J Lacy, and J Stone, 1724.

Lewis, CS, *The Magician's Nephew*. **The Chronicles of Narnia** #1. 1955. London, Fontana Lions, 1980. ISBN 9780006716679.

Lewis, CS, *The Last Battle*. **The Chronicles of Narnia** #7. 1956. London, Fontana Lions, 1980. ISBN 9780006716693.

Ling, Peter, *Doctor Who: The Mind Robber*. **The Target Doctor Who Library** #115. London, WH Allen, 1986. ISBN 9780426202868.

Lyons, Steve, *Conundrum*. **Doctor Who: The New Adventures**. London, Virgin Publishing Ltd, 1994. ISBN 9780426204084.

Lyons, Steve, *Head Games*. **Doctor Who: The New Adventures**. London, Virgin Publishing Ltd, 1995. ISBN 9780426204541.

Moorcock, Michael, *A Nomad of the Time Streams*. London, Orion Publishing, 1996. ISBN 9781857984484.

Myles, LM, *The Ambassadors of Death*. **The Black Archive** #3. Edinburgh, Obverse Books, 2016. ISBN 9781909031395.

Nesbit, E, *The Story of the Treasure Seekers: Being the Adventures of the Bastable Children in Search of a Fortune*. London, T Fisher Unwin, 1899.

Nesbit, E, *Five Children and It*. London, T Fisher Unwin, 1902.

Nesbit, E, *The Railway Children*. Wells Gardner, Darton & Co, 1906.

Orwell, George, *Essays*. London, Everyman, 2002. ISBN 9781857152425.

Perryman, Neil, and Sue Perryman, *The Miserable Git*. **The Wife In Space,** #1. Sue Me Books, 2015. ISBN 9781310464195.

Roberts, Adam, *The History of Science Fiction*. **Palgrave Histories of Literature**. London, Palgrave Macmillan, 2005. ISBN 9780230546912.

Rostand, Edmond, *Cyrano de Bergerac: A Heroic Comedy in Five Acts*. 1897. Christopher Fry, trans, Oxford, Oxford University Press, 1996. ISBN 9780192824240.

Sandifer, Philip, *Patrick Troughton*. **TARDIS Eruditorum: A Critical History of Doctor Who** #2. Newtown, Eruditorum Press, 2012. ISBN 9781479389063.

Shearman, Robert, and Toby Hadoke, *The 60s*. **Running Through Corridors: Rob and Toby's Marathon Watch of Doctor Who**, #1. Des Moines, Mad Norwegian Press, 2010, ISBN 9781935234067.

Swift, Jonathan, *Travels into Several Remote Nations of the World, in Four Parts: By Lemuel Gulliver, First a Surgeon, and then a Captain of Several Ships*. 1726. Revised ed, Dublin, George Faulkner, 1735.

Wood, Tat, and Lawrence Miles, *1963-1966: Seasons 1 to 3*. **About Time: The Unauthorized Guide to Doctor Who** #1. Des Moines, Mad Norwegian Press, 2006. ISBN 9780975944608.

Wood, Tat, and Lawrence Miles, *1966-1969: Seasons 4 to 6*. **About Time: The Unauthorized Guide to Doctor Who** #2 Des Moines, Mad Norwegian Press, 2007. ISBN 9780975944615.

Wood, Tat, and Lawrence Miles, *1975-1979: Seasons 12 to 17*. **About Time: The Unauthorized Guide to Doctor Who** #4. Des Moines, Mad Norwegian Press, 2004. ISBN 9780975944639.

Periodicals

Boys of England. EJ Brett, 1867-1900.

Doctor Who: The Complete History. London, Hachette Partworks.

> #13 *Stories 45-47: The Mind Robber, The Invasion and The Krotons*, 2015.

Doctor Who Magazine (DWM). Marvel UK, Panini, BBC, 1979-.

> Gray, Scott, and Adrian Salmon, 'Character Assassin'. DWM #311, cover date December 2001.

The Eagle. Hulton Press, 1950-69.

The Gem. Amalgamated Press, 1907-39.

The Magnet. Amalgamated Press, 1908-40.

Moore, Alan, and Kevin O'Neill, **The League of Extraordinary Gentlemen**. ABC, Wildstorm, DC Comics, Top Shelf Comics, 1999-.

Television

Alice In Wonderland. BBC, 1966.

The Adventures of Sir Lancelot. Sapphire Films, 1956-57.

The Avengers. ABC, 1961-69.

Batman. Greenaway Productions, 20th Century Fox Television, 1966-68.

Crossroads. ATV, Central, 1964-88.

Doctor Who. BBC, 1963-.

EastEnders. BBC, 1985-.

Grandstand. BBC, 1958-2007.

The Monkees. Raybert Productions, 1966-68.

The Newcomers. BBC, 1965-69.

Out of the Unknown. BBC, 1965-71.

> *The Prophet*, 1967.

Paul Temple. BBC, ZDF, 1969-71.

The Quatermass Experiment. BBC, 1953.

Quatermass II. BBC, 1955.

Quatermass and the Pit. BBC, 1958-59.

Star Trek. Desilu Productions, Norway Corporation, Paramount Television, 1966-69.

The Railway Children. BBC, 1957.

The Railway Children. BBC, 1968.

The Simpsons. Gracie Films, 20th Century Fox Television, 1989-.

The Three Musketeers. BBC, 1966

Whirligig. BBC, 1950-56.

Z Cars. BBC, 1962-78.

Film

The Childhood of Jack Harkaway. Thanhouser Company, 1910.

Fisher, Terrence, dir, *The Gorgon*. Hammer, 1964.

Flemyng, Gordon, dir, *Dr Who and the Daleks*. AARU Productions, Amicus Productions, 1965.

Flemyng, Gordon, dir, *Daleks: Invasion Earth 2150 AD*. AARU Productions, Amicus Productions, 1966.

Jeffries, Lionel, dir, *The Railway Children*. EMI Elstree, 1970.

Logan, Joshua, dir, *Camelot*. Warner Bros, Seven Arts, 1967.

Stevenson, Robert, dir, *Blackbeard's Ghost*. Walt Disney Productions, 1968.

Audio CD

Bovey, Simon, *City of Spires*. **Doctor Who**. Big Finish Productions, 2010.

Cook, Peter, *Peter Cook Presents The Misty Mr. Wisty*. 1965. Sound Entertainment Ltd, 2005.

Dorney, John, *The Crooked Man*. **Doctor Who: The Fourth Doctor Adventures**. Big Finish Productions, 2014

Edwards, Barnaby, *The Wreck of the Titan*. **Doctor Who**. Big Finish Productions, 2010.

Maddox, Mike, *Legend of the Cybermen*. **Doctor Who**. Big Finish Productions, 2010.

Ross, Marty, *Night's Black Agents*. **Doctor Who: The Companion Chronicles**. Big Finish Productions 2010.

Web

'BBC Genome Project'. http://genome.ch.bbc.co.uk/. Accessed 25 March 2016.

'Boys of England [Electronic Resource]: A Magazine of Sport, Sensation, Fun, and Instruction'. https://searchworks.stanford.edu/view/10549458. Accessed 25 March 2016.

TARDIS Data Core. http://tardis.wikia.com/wiki/Doctor_Who_Wiki.

'The Mind Robber (TV story)'. http://tardis.wikia.com/wiki/The_Mind_Robber_(TV_story). Accessed 23 May 2016.

Hayward, Anthony, 'Peter Ling'. *The Independent*. 26 September 2006. http://www.independent.co.uk/news/obituaries/peter-ling-417668.html. Accessed 25 March 2016.

Ness, Mari, 'Fighting Capitalism Through Children: *The Story of the Treasure-Seekers*'. 28 July 2011. http://www.tor.com/2011/07/28/capitalism-it-is-depressing-the-story-of-the-treasure-seekers/. Accessed 25 March 2016.

Nicholson, Mervyn, 'CS Lewis and the Scholarship of Imagination in E Nesbit and Rider Haggard'. Renascence: Essays on Values in Literature. Marquette University Press, 1998. http://www.thefreelibrary.com/c.+s.+lewis+and+the+scholarship+of+imagination+in+e.+nesbit+and+rider...-a054099033. Accessed 25 March 2016.

Stevens, Alan, 'Donald Tosh Interview'. Kaldor City. www.kaldorcity.com/people/dtinterview.html. Accessed 25 March 2016.

Vidal, Gore, 'The Writing of E Nesbit'. *The New York Review of Books*, 3 December 1964. http://www.nybooks.com/articles/1964/12/03/the-writing-of-e-nesbit/. Accessed 25 March 2016.

Williams, Abigail, and Kate O'Connor, 'Jonathan Swift and *Gulliver's Travels*'. Writers Inspire. http://writersinspire.org/content/jonathan-swift-gullivers-travels. Accessed 25 March 2016.

BIOGRAPHY

Andrew Hickey is a writer, unsuccessful musician, and perennial third-place political candidate. When not losing elections he writes books on subjects including **Doctor Who**, superhero comics, 1960s harmony pop music, and the tenuous connections that can be found between those subjects if you look hard enough.

His first novel, *Faction Paradox: Head of State,* was published by Obverse Books in 2015. He lives in Manchester, England, with a very tolerant wife and a less tolerant Jack Russell.